All our love.

Emm x

Sophie &
Alexander.

Simon

INNOCENT

ABROAD

Best wishes.
Andrew

With all our love
Sandy & Margaret.

lots of love
Jane
x

Lots of love
from
Alec & Catherine.

love Jean.

With fondest love,
Andrew & Dawn xx.

INNOCENT ABROAD

The Travels of
Miss Hannah Hauxwell

HANNAH HAUXWELL
with BARRY COCKCROFT

ARROW BOOKS

Also by Barry Cockcroft

Hannah in Yorkshire
The Ways of a Yorkshire Dale
The Dale that Died
Princes of the Plough
A Romany Summer
A Celebration of Yorkshire
Seasons of My Life
Daughter of the Dales
Hannah: The Complete Story

Published by Arrow Books Limited
20 Vauxhall Bridge Road, London SW1V 2SA

An imprint of Random House UK Limited

London Melbourne Sydney Auckland Johannesburg
and agencies throughout the world

First published in 1991 by Random Century Group

Arrow edition 1992

© 1991 by Tracestar

Colour photographs of Hannah Hauxwell by
Mostafa Hammuri
Design by Behram Kapadia
Set in Palatino by SX Composing Ltd, Raleigh, Essex
Printed and bound in Great Britain by
Butler & Tanner Ltd, Frome and London

ISBN 0 09 997170 4

Line engravings on pages 13, 37, 53, 69, 83, 93, 107, 115, 127, 141, 151,
169, 181 from The Mansell Collection

Contents

Preface

The Beginnings of an Odyssey

The Odyssey of Hannah Hauxwell had two beginnings.

The first blossomed briefly in 1989 at a certain Chinese restaurant in Leeds where for more than a dozen years many acclaimed Yorkshire Television documentary programmes first took shape on flimsy paper table napkins. Indeed, one YTV cutting room wall featured a display of tattered, sauce-splattered scraps bearing scarcely legible programme structures scrawled out with borrowed ballpoints. But they were as frail as butterfly wings and disintegrated long ago.

A great pity, since the early history of one of the most successful documentary teams ever spawned by British television was writ thus.

One of the first to emerge in this manner was a programme called 'Too Long a Winter', which turned into a seven napkin job as sequences were juggled endlessly around film of a white-haired lady with a curiously hypnotic voice who dressed in outrageously romantic rags.

Name of Hannah Hauxwell.

We – that is, the writer of this piece (who produced and directed the programme) and the head of documentaries – suspected they had an alluring personality in Miss Hauxwell and decided to chance making her the pivot of the film. Clearly, she could communicate, the camera had definitely fallen in love with her and what a life she led! Almost beyond belief. So hard a life that she looked ten . . . no . . . maybe twenty years older than the forty-six she had struggled on her comfortless farm on an income of £280 a year. No electricity, no water on tap, totally alone in a half abandoned dale . . . and drawing her drinking water from a turgid stream where her single cow, which produced one calf a year for market, squelched around doing whatever it pleased.

Yes . . . undoubtedly a good story in the journalistic sense . . . and the lady could certainly deliver it.

Gradually, those who worked on the editing of the film began to realize that something extraordinary was afoot. Silent figures from other cutting rooms started to haunt the shadows at the rear of cutting room five, watching the images flickering endlessly to and fro on the Steenbeck editing machine.

It was the speech mannerisms of Hannah that initially caught people's attention. The words appeared to float from her lips like a progression of musical chords. And at the same time she projected a certain inexplicable aura – her face, already glowing rosily from the elements, was further illuminated by the light reflecting from her pure white, fine-spun hair. Overall it created an ethereal impression . . . angelic, almost!

'Too Long a Winter' was offered to the British public late at night on 31 January 1973. The effect was explosive. All Yorkshire Television telephone lines were jammed for two days and nights, the GPO organized special deliveries direct to the documentary department in sacks and the amazed programme makers were obliged to hastily organize a team to deal with it all. They tried to form a protective ring around Hannah as hundreds of people set out to locate her, desperate for a look or a word as though they required confirmation that what they had seen on their screens was truly a person on the same planet.

At first it was feared that the programme would ruin the poor woman and overwhelm her life by sheer weight of numbers. But the difficulty of locating and then reaching her well-hidden home helped to deter all but the most determined of pilgrims. Those that did plunge through the bog that rings the front of Low Birk Hatt, except in high summer, mostly approached her with polite deference, sometimes with the sort of awe one associates with an introduction to royalty. One middle-aged lady was observed dashing away from Hannah exclaiming 'I touched her! . . . I touched her!'

But Hannah Bayles Tallentire Hauxwell turned out to possess the wisdom and ability to not only cope with the dramatic change to her status, but to effortlessly and innocently create an image which has endured and grown for two decades. Innocence is the key factor with Hannah, allied to a saintly disposition which allowed her to accept the circumstances Fate had dealt her for so many years, without a word of reproach.

The single recurring theme in all the letters and messages sent to her – and her fame swiftly spread to millions overseas as her film gathered a world-wide reputation and a clutch of awards – was that people felt they owed her a debt of gratitude. Her story and her attitude to life had inspired them to review their own lives, to 'count their blessings' (a phrase used again and again) and to face the future with new resolve and purpose.

Thus Hannah, the person who had the best excuse in Britain to feel sorry for herself but never did, became the great eradicator of self-pity.

In the meantime, the Hannah Hauxwell saga rolled onwards irresistibly. Ceaseless media attention, more documentaries and books about her life followed in the wake of 'Too Long a Winter'. The bestselling *Hannah in Yorkshire* preceded 'Hannah Goes to Town', the film of Hannah's first visit to London where she attended the Women of the Year lunch as a guest of honour. Then came a series of short regional films, such as the one made about her second visit to the capital to attend a Buckingham Palace garden party.

There were times when those associated with these film and literary endeavours fully expected the public interest in Hannah to eventually wane. But the chorus asking for more of the same grew steadily in volume as the years went by. The number of letters from viewers pleading for repeats of the documentaries (many asking for earlier transmission times for the sake of the children and elderly folk) broke all records, and continues to this day.

So another documentary film was carefully prepared, spanning several years of Hannah's spartan life at Low Birk Hatt and concluding with her sorrowful departure to her cottage in Cotherstone. Just before it was transmitted, Hannah's book, *Seasons of My Life: The Story of a Solitary Daleswoman* was published. It became an instant bestseller, reaching the number one position and remaining in the Non-fiction Top Ten for months.

'A Winter Too Many' was screened in October 1989. It was hailed as the most successful documentary of the year. Despite being scheduled after 10.30 at night, it recorded an audience of well over six million – phenomenal!

So there it was – confirmation, if confirmation was really

needed, that Hannah Hauxwell's appeal was as powerful as ever. And she was more than just a celebrity . . . she had become an icon, a point of reference for legions of people. And she spanned the generations and national frontiers. Among those who queue for hours to meet Hannah when she makes publicized appearances – to sign her books, for instance – were young people who were scarcely out of their cradles when 'Too Long a Winter' was first transmitted in 1973. And in both Norway and Sweden the response to 'A Winter Too Many' when it reached their television screens in 1990 was so profound that it was swiftly repeated.

Which all led to a celebratory lunch at the same, unfailingly excellent Chinese restaurant in Leeds (the Jumbo, for those who wish to know), attended by the same pair who structured the original film on paper napkins almost twenty years before: the writer of this piece and his chief, who by then had ascended to the position of Director of Programmes. No furious scribbling this time, just a remembrance of times past and an acknowledgement of just how fortunate we had been to find Hannah.

Naturally, we discussed the feasibility of more filming with the lady. The Great British Public was hammering at the gates yet again, demanding a follow-up to 'A Winter Too Many'. But the conclusion was obvious: there was no way anyone could make a documentary about a pensioner living a life of comfortable retirement in a cottage with all modern conveniences, such as central heating and hot running water. And an ex-directory telephone! It was quite another matter when she and her animals were fighting for survival in furious blizzards, alone, a thousand feet up a desolate dale and breaking ice to get drinking water.

But what about Hannah's supreme talent to communicate . . . that was something to consider. There was a moment's reflection as plates were cleared and the last of the wine poured.

'Unless . . . ' said this writer, 'Hannah wanted to travel . . . to totally leave her comfortable environment and go out to meet new challenges in places strange to her. She has mentioned an inclination to travel one day if all the circumstances were right. If we did think about a follow-up along those lines . . . a one-off, or even a series . . . the title suggests itself, does it not.'

'Innocent Abroad . . .'

This beguiling prospect was savoured for a minute or two, and then a consensus opinion was arrived at. Perhaps . . . but maybe not . . . unless, of course, the momentum came from Hannah herself. Then we might be able to look at it seriously.

That was the first, hesitant step towards The Odyssey of Hannah Hauxwell. There was to be a lapse of several months before the next. It occurred when the final chapter of Hannah's latest literary triumph, *Daughter of the Dales: The World of Hannah Hauxwell*, was being written. The last page of the manuscript contained the following passage:

'Looking ahead, I suppose travel would be nice, if only the opportunity arose and I had the courage to go with it. I have a wish to go to Paris . . .'

Shortly after publication, Hannah gently announced that she was seriously considering an invitation to stay with some new friends . . . at their villa in Spain!

'Hannah,' said this writer. 'You do realize that if you decide to venture forth like that, to cross the ocean to foreign parts, board a plane even, then I really should be there with a film unit.'

'Oh, yes,' said Hannah, with that smile which seems to illuminate everything for a hundred yards around.

'I suppose so . . .'

BARRY COCKCROFT

1

Paris, My First Love

When I was in my teens, there was a kind lady who lived up the dale at West Friar House called Mrs Isobel Bainbridge who used to lend books to me. It was she who loaned me *Little Women*, the first book I read to enjoy. Now, she was a schoolmistress before she married and had actually been to Paris when she was still a maiden lady – Miss Roberts – and brought back some little books about the place with lots of illustrations. One day she gave me those to read and I was very taken by them. So, as far as places abroad are concerned Paris has always been my first love, so to speak. The Champs-Elysées, the Arc de Triomphe, the Opera House, Notre-Dame, and the Louvre . . . they all seemed such desirable and romantic places to a young girl, but I always thought my fancy to see them would be just a dream . . . just castles in the air.

You know, it's all right to have a few dreams, as long as you don't set your heart on things happening to make them come true.

In my young days, and for many years after that, opportunities for me to travel were strictly limited. Just day trips with the school and chapel to places like Redcar or Saltburn, which didn't involve very long journeys. But they weren't always happy occasions for me because I was such a sickly traveller in those days. Even on the weekly bus from Baldersdale to Barnard Castle I would often be queasy, especially when we went over the humped-back bridges. I prefer to travel by rail, and recall a train journey to Scarborough once, which was nice – except it took such a long time to get there. It's the only time I've ever been to Scarborough, and it was such a while ago that all I can remember about the place is that it had a lot of steps to go up and down.

The furthest I ever went in my youth was a day trip to Loch Lomond, and a very long day it turned out to be. Alec Howson from Barnard Castle, who did all our trips, got a new bus just after the Second World War, and the late Mr Ernie High, from Briscoe in Baldersdale, suggested he did something special to mark the occasion, so Loch Lomond was chosen. We met at Clove Lodge, the farm above Low Birk Hatt, at six in the morning and arrived back at four the following morning. Alec drove all the way – I don't know how he did it – and I recall he had

The view over Paris from Montmartre.

some trouble by-passing Glasgow. I had my own problems too, with my inclination to travel sickness, but I do have clear memories of miles and miles of moorland and fir trees and little one-storey houses with arched windows. We couldn't stay long at Loch Lomond, but we did have time for a brew of tea. Somebody was worried about whether or not the tea would be any good, but all was well when the late Mr John Iceton of Willoughby Hall announced that it would be because a whole quarter pound had gone into the can!

Of course, I've always found the thought of travel quite fascinating but when I was a one-woman farmer it didn't allow, either financially or any other way. Indeed, there were only certain times of the year when it was possible to leave my animals, especially when I was milking them by hand, morning and evening. Only when I retired from farming two years ago, when I made up sixty-two years, and came to Cotherstone did the opportunity to travel occur, and I have been to London a few times, which I always enjoy, and I've journeyed by car quite a lot locally, and even to the Midlands to bookshops to sign copies of my books.

In fact, I have travelled far more in the last two years than at any other time in my life, but I never really contemplated going to foreign parts . . . crossing an ocean! Up to now, passports have been something that other people needed, not me. I never dreamt for one moment that I would possess one.

Although I am not as prone to sickness as I once was I do have certain reservations. I am neither a flier nor a swimmer. I know it will be necessary to go across the Channel – for preference, by the shortest distance possible. And I know there will still be plenty of water to drown me fifty times over, but I am prepared to risk it.

However, I do not wish to fly. A lot of people do, of course, and statistics tend to prove that flying is safer than driving on the road. And there's the funny thing about it, because people come to me on a regular basis and take me here there and everywhere by motor car and I never have any qualms.

But no . . . I have no desire to enter an aeroplane, the lesser evil will be the boat.

Such firmly stated preferences by Hannah certainly helped to fashion the framework of her impending travel plans. She clearly made a classic Innocent Abroad, and since the exclusion of travel by air, the style would have to be distinctly Victorian – by boats and trains exclusively.

Then the realization dawned that this mode would be absolutely right for Hannah. She is by nature and inclination a Victorian, locked in a time-warp and exhibiting all the characteristics of the maiden ladies of a century ago. Her attitudes, mannerisms and speech patterns are more in tune with that elegant and deliberate era when the world progressed at a much more leisurely pace than in the tearaway twentieth century.

Hannah, then, was spiritually akin to those intrepid Victorian ladies who were beginning to defy the accepted convention that travel without a male guardian was unthinkable. Wayward women they were dubbed, but a fashion for foreign travel, hitherto the preserve of the upper classes, had been flourishing for the lower orders since the middle of the nineteeth century.

And the person who began it all was, oddly enough, the Secretary of the Leicester Temperance Society.

Name of Thomas Cook.

His mission in life was to fight the Demon Drink. And he came up with the idea that travel might be a tempting alternative to the tavern. So 150 years ago he began to charter trains and arrange trips to places like Scarborough and Liverpool – exciting enough places at the time for the newly emerging middle classes. They were hugely successful, so he courageously raised his sights and began to take his clients across the Channel. Thomas Cook thus became the world's first Excursionist, the veritable father of today's massive travel industry.

Because of Mr Cook's well-advertised high moral stance and because he personally escorted most of his early tours abroad, the male guardians of maiden ladies reluctantly conceded that he provided a measure of protection against the unknown perils of foreign parts. And the ladies came to him in petticoated droves.

One of the originals who accompanied Mr Cook on his first venture abroad was Miss Jemima Morrell, like Hannah a maiden lady from Yorkshire. She travelled to Paris and the Alps and the journal of her experiences merited publication.

So, it was in the same spirit that the initial leg of Hannah's first venture overseas was arranged. She would follow in Miss Jemima's footsteps, even staying at the same hotels, if possible. There would be other Victorian ladies to emulate (and how they could write) as Hannah's tour progressed, but Miss Jemima set the pace and the style.

The preparation at Belle Vue Cottage, Cotherstone, where Hannah has been living in contented if exceedingly busy retirement since she tearfully vacated Low Birk Hatt, Baldersdale, in the winter of 1988, consumed all her nervous energy for months. Applying for a passport, worrying about leaving her little terrier, Timmy, and just coming to terms with the idea psychologically caused her some sleepless nights.

And then there was the question of her wardrobe! The public image of Hannah has her dressed in wellies, and exotic layers of rags, and she has shown scant inclination to change it since she

Thomas Cook, c1850, the world's first Excursionist, left, and Miss Jemima Morrell, the pathfinder, right. *Courtesy of Thomas Cook Archives*

moved into the genteel, twinset-and-pearls atmosphere of Cother-stone society.

Yes, I have had a good bit of advice from well-meaning friends that I was now living in a village, had no need to wear my farm clothes, and must smarten myself up a bit. But I am afraid it has fallen on deaf ears somewhat, because I am happier in my old things. There are certain occasions when one must dress more conventionally, and there was one notable incident when I was, sadly, recently attending the funeral of a cousin of mine, and I met an acquaintance who seemed to be in a bit of a hurry, perhaps a trifle distant. Then a day or two later she came to see me and said she was awfully sorry but she hadn't recognized me at the funeral because I was dressed up! I was much amused about that.

Mind, although I go about in my old rags I do like nice things

Notre-Dame.
The Mansell Collection

and I have a whole new wardrobe for my travels. Some dresses have been especially made for me, including three or four lovely long creations. I have never worn a long dress before and I'm a bit afraid of tripping up and coming a cropper. I'll just have to learn how to move properly when I've got them on. The shoes were a problem because my feet are a bit oddly shaped, through wearing wellington boots night and day for years, I suppose. High heels are out of the question, but two or three pairs of nice flat shoes were hunted down eventually. And I have a selection of beautiful hats – I like hats – and a very posh camel coat, almost like a cape it is.

I think my favourite is a long flowing purple dress. It is a colour I particularly fancy. Indeed, I feel like Cinderella going to the ball when I survey my new clothes. I know that it wasn't Cinderella who turned into a pumpkin when the clock struck, but it might happen to me!

Hannah Hauxwell's adventure began in classic style early one morning in Victoria Station from which the boat train for Paris has been leaving for well over a century. The basic structure of the place has been changed little over the years, and the atmosphere is always charged with the excitement of impending foreign travel. The ghosts of Thomas Cook, Miss Jemima, *et al.*, must have been hovering in the great vaulted roof, looking on benignly as a resplendent Hannah, camel coat flowing behind her, matching hat at a rakish angle, wide eyes darting everywhere, trotted alongside her luggage and chatted animatedly, as she always does, to a jovial West Indian porter who rejoiced in the curiously appropriate name of Mr Pilgrim.

She told him how surprised she was at the vastness of his workplace and how impressed she was with the 'beautiful tiled floor'.

From then on everything was a new experience for Hannah. As the boat train progressed towards Dover, she saw the south of England for the first time and was much taken by the oast houses by the hop fields of Kent. Then came the first challenge – her first sight of the Channel and a seagoing boat, the very large and splendid new Sealink vessel, the *Fantasia*. As she prepared to board, Hannah looked up at it with a mixture of awe and apprehension.

It was so big it took me some time to figure out just how to get on to it, and I was a bit nervous about the prospect of being seasick. I have never been on an ocean before, unless you can count a trip some kind friends took me on years ago on the ferry between North Shields and South Shields. But I took some medication, a couple of tablets, and I'd brought a lemon with me. That's an old gypsy remedy against queasy feelings – in Baldersdale we used to be visited every year by the Romanies, remember. Miss Jemima, my distinguished predecessor on this journey, recommended a 'specific for the malady of blackcurrant preserve and brandy', but that just didn't appeal. I tried to keep my fingers crossed, too, on boarding the *Fantasia* but had to use my hand to keep my hat on my head because it was blowing a bit.

It took me some time to get used to the scale and comfort of the boat – I had no idea that a ferry boat could be so big and luxurious. A kind gentleman presented me with a lovely bouquet of flowers as I boarded, and ordered a pot of tea and a plate of sandwiches. That was most welcome as I had been advised not to indulge myself with a rich breakfast, but I thought I had better have something in my stomach. I watched the white cliffs of Dover slipping away and thought of that song which was so popular on the wireless during the war years, and it wasn't long before I was recognized by my fellow passengers who had seen the television programmes, and had read the books. They kindly came over to my table for a chat and were most impressed to hear of my travel plans. And the gentleman who gave me the flowers arrived to say that the Captain would be pleased to see me on the bridge. We had to go up quite a few staircases and I noticed then that the boat was rocking a bit, but I was still most surprised when the Captain, a Mr John Roberts, told me there was a force seven gale blowing! He asked me if I had suffered any seasickness and I was able to assure him with much pleasure that I had certainly expected to, what with my previous susceptibility, but had not felt the slightest discomfort.

Perhaps an even bigger surprise was the sight of the French coast when I was on the bridge. We appeared to be almost on top of it, yet the journey had seemed so short. We had been at sea for only an hour or so. It must have taken much longer when poor Miss Jemima bounced across the Channel all those years ago, and I do hope that Mr Cook was immune to the malady since he must have spent a fair proportion of his working life at sea.

It was a big thrill for me to set foot on foreign soil for the very first time and to have my brand new passport examined. I had had the photograph taken at one of those little booths at Darlington Bus Station – I needed a bit of assistance since it was somewhat complicated – but it was a good enough likeness to pass muster. The rail journey between Calais and Paris was very comfortable. The French train was quite impressive – I do hope our government will spend a bit more money improving our own railways – and I noticed a significant difference between the French countryside and our own. There appeared to be no fences or dry-stone walls between the fields. I wondered how they know which bit of land belongs to whom. There were whole stretches without an obvious boundary. And the land, even the gardens, came right up to the railway in some cases. There is very little wastage of ground there, not as much as we have in Britain anyhow. I also noticed some nice beasties in the fields, some Charollais, of course, and a few Friesians.

The arrival in Paris was something special for me, as I knew it would be. All those years I had been imagining what it would be like, and it lived up to expectations. My first glimpse of the Champs-Elysées and the Arc de Triomphe will always stay with me – someone said they thought I was going to jump clean out of the taxi!

The manager himself, a Mr Patrice Puvilland, was waiting to greet me at the George V Hotel. I should say Monsieur Puvilland, of course – I'm afraid I know only about half a dozen words in French – bonjour, bon voyage, monsieur, madame, mademoiselle, and that's it. But I consider French to be a very charming tongue – very musical. I try hard to listen, but they do seem to speak very quickly. Fortunately everyone at the hotel, including the porters and the waiters, seemed very fluent in English. They were most attentive, and I went straight to my room – well, it was a suite really – because the journey and all the excitement had made me very tired. I had even fallen asleep for a while on the train. I told them that a pot of tea would be most welcome, and as I waited for it I recalled what Miss Jemima had written in her journal when she and her travelling companions had done exactly the same more than a hundred years ago: 'We sat in judgement for the first time on French tea, which we pronounced to be truly peculiar.' Well, mine turned out to be a bit better than Miss Jemima's – or so I imagine. It could have done to be a mite hotter, but I enjoyed it. At least the cups were big, which I like. All in all English tea is the best, but one has to balance that judgement by conceding that the French are superior when it comes to coffee. But my surroundings were truly magnificent, and all the furniture seemed to be antique and most attractive. There was even a carved bust, on a cabinet, with curly hair, which gazed at me all the time but I couldn't give it a name because I never did work out whether it was a lady or a gentleman. The entire hotel was very grand and spacious, and beautifully furnished, with lots of paintings. I heard there was even a Renoir somewhere, but no one seemed to know exactly where. In the manager's office, maybe. The place reminded me strongly of our own Savoy Hotel, where I had been privileged to stay once when I was invited to the Women of the Year lunch back in the seventies.

Next day Hannah launched herself decorously on Paris, moving at her own pace – that is to say with measured step, and many considered pauses – to properly appreciate the glories of this most elegant of capital cities. There was to be no straining of the leash, in the manner of the average tourist. Miss Hannah, like the Victorian maiden ladies who preceded her, was not to be rushed. First she became well acquainted with the Champs-Elysées, and made a slow-moving figure which contrasted sharply with the customary bustle of traffic and pedestrians racing to the next destination. She was wide-eyed and wearing another new hat to celebrate the occasion.

Hannah was particularly taken by the Arc de Triomphe, noting how superbly it had been positioned and protected in that no other building intruded to diminish its magnificence. It was set always against a background of Parisian sky, and during her entire stay in Paris Hannah never failed to become alert with pleasure whenever the Arc de Triomphe came into view as she criss-crossed the city by taxi. Invariably she found something unexpected to say about every new visual experience. That probably stems from her background and upbringing. People who live in more remote areas have different points of reference to the standard urban dweller. They can always see things, or at least interpret them, in a distinctive fashion and Hannah is a classic example of this particular minority.

Hannah's second night in Paris was a gala occasion and it led to an entirely unexpected incident. A magnificent example of Gallic charm and persuasion culminated with Hannah breaking – well, bending really – a rule she had adhered to all her life. Concerning alcoholic beverages. She had been invited by the Bateaux Mouche Company to join one of their dinner cruises down the Seine. Even for widely travelled people with sophisticated tastes this is quite an experience – the boats are lavishly appointed and the entire cruise is executed with tremendous style. Hannah prepared carefully for this special night.

I chose to wear one of the nicest garments in my new collection. It was a very long dress made from a multicoloured tweed material manufactured in Carlisle. And I was assured that they sent a lot of this particular fabric to French fashion houses – even Coco Chanel, a big name in Paris apparently. So I thought it would be most appropriate for the cruise down the Seine. It also had a rather pretty white blouse with a big collar edged in broderie anglaise. Since I was still learning how to walk in it without falling, I was a bit concerned when I went down the gangplank to the boat, and sure enough it got mixed up with my big feet and I almost took a tumble. But there was a nice gentleman in a dress suit and tails who caught me and managed to get me safely to my table. Such a beautiful setting, too, and all the tables lit by little oil lamps fed by a lilac-coloured oil. It reminded me of winter nights back at Low Birk Hatt when oil lamps were all I had to light the place. And, before we set off, this very large French gentleman, Monsieur Bruel, came to meet me. I think he was the owner of the boat. Well, he was most charming and spoke English very well, with that lovely French accent. He told me he had been in England during the war, having escaped to join the Free French forces. But for some reason he did not appear to hold a good opinion of the late General de Gaulle, his leader. He then proceeded to open a bottle – I think it was some-

A memorable dinner cruise on the Seine.

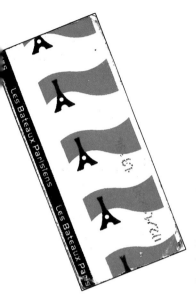

thing like champagne because there was a pronounced pop when the cork came out – and poured some into my glass. I tried to tell him that I didn't touch alcohol, never had in my life. But he didn't seem to understand. He was obviously very proud of it, saying it had come from his very own vineyard. Now there I was, a guest in another country and, eventually, as I did not wish to give offence, I had just a sip. To return his toast, you understand. But I didn't have any more after that.

Everything about that night was memorable. There were enormous banks of lights on the side of the boat to illuminate the places we passed. The waters of the Seine shimmered like jewels and the Eiffel Tower seemed to be constructed of pure gold. And the bridges . . . well, they are a legend, are they not. So romantic. And they played appropriate music, particularly when we came to Notre-Dame, which was a sight to inspire anyone and the air was filled with Handel's 'Halleluja' Chorus.

Me and the Mona Lisa.

Outside the Louvre
pyramid.

From then on my trip to Paris was a bit of a whirl, just one vivid experience piling on top of the other. Next day I was taken to the Louvre and saw that glass pyramid they built recently as a new entrance. I read somewhere that it has been somewhat controversial, with some people hating it and others liking it, and I tend to feel that it somehow doesn't fit in with all those magnificent, traditional buildings all around it.

The Louvre itself is a huge place, much bigger than I expected. You would need a whole week to do it justice, and I wish there had been more time. Of course, I was most anxious to see the *Mona Lisa*. Some people have said that I bear more than a slight resemblance to that enigmatic lady, but I must confess that I didn't see it myself when I finally came face to face with her. Now it was a big thrill to see the most famous and valuable picture in the whole world and I am told that people have been moved to the point of committing suicide over it. But I have to say that I wasn't drawn to it. I saw other paintings nearby that I would prefer to possess.

Later on I did come face to face with a picture of myself when I went up the hill to Montmartre, to the Place du Tertre, a tiny little square fringed with trees which is full of artists painting and trying to sell their pictures to the tourists. One or two of them do instant portraits and I sat for a very romantic-looking gentleman who had curly hair and a goatee beard and looked very much the part of the struggling artist.

The weather was unseasonably cold when you consider it was April and we were in Paris – not like the sentiments of the song at all – so I kept my hat and coat on as he drew my likeness in crayon. It took him less than half an hour and he didn't say much, probably because he knew very little English and he was also very cold. And I have to say that I was flattered when he showed me the result because he made me look much younger than I actually am. But I imagine he does that for everyone. Quite a crowd gathered to watch the artist working, including a very nice family from the West Riding of Yorkshire, who recognized me. They took pictures of me and we had a nice chat. Apparently, the lady had waited six weeks before it was her turn at the local library to borrow one of my books.

Just round the corner from the Place du Tertre, and dominating all that part of Montmartre is Sacré-Coeur, a huge church built out of a lovely white stone. You can see its dome from all over Paris. I found it a trifle disappointing inside – rather dark and shut off – and not at all as impressive as our own York Minster. But the view over the city from its big, wide steps was really something, and I did enjoy watching the youngsters who congregate around Sacré-Coeur, playing their guitars and laughing and singing. It seems to be a kind of meeting place for students and young travellers.

On the steps of the Sacré-Coeur, overlooking Montmartre.

Of course, it is situated in the Pigalle area which I am told has a wild side to it. So it would naturally attract the younger element. I found it very interesting to drive through, and saw the Moulin-Rouge, the world-famous night-club which has a big red wind-mill on the top. Years ago I saw a film about Toulouse-Lautrec

A flattering portrait in the Place du Tertre.

which I believe featured the Moulin-Rouge, but I did not feel I wanted to attend one of the performances there. I think the style of the show would not have suited me. I consider that the human body, however beautiful, is better covered with nice clothing, leaving something to the imagination.

My evenings in Paris were spent enjoying their renowned cuisine, although there was one unusual aspect to that. To begin with I ate dinner in my suite at the George V and for two nights running enjoyed their grilled sole *meunière*. I don't know how on earth they achieved such a tasty dish. The fish had little brown latticework criss-crossed over it, and it was accompanied by a lovely sauce and such nice vegetables. But the last night I ended up experiencing very different food because our cameraman, Mostafa Hammuri, who I call the Great Mostafa, found that there was a Lebanese restaurant directly opposite the hotel. He was born in what was Palestine and greatly misses the traditional food of the Middle East so he ate there as often as possible, and persuaded me to try it. He said that poor Beirut, so badly disfigured by all the upset and strife, used to be the Paris of the Middle East and that their cooking was similarly renowned. I found it very tasty, a nice change. Something called *falafels* I liked, apparently made from chick peas with herbs and spices and deep fried which Mostafa used to have for school lunch every day. And I had some sausages made from lamb – very unusual. But wherever you go, Paris is the place for fine food. Be it breakfast, lunch or dinner, I don't think I've tasted better.

Facing up to boarding a boat and crossing an ocean for the first time was an obvious challenge, but towards the end of her stay in Paris another, less expected psychological obstacle reared up – quite literally. A trip up the Eiffel Tower had always been on the essential list of things to do in Paris, but Hannah had been curiously withdrawn whenever the very symbol of Paris was mentioned. And her companions were distinctly taken aback when, during an interview filmed as she sat for her portrait, she reacted in an uncharacteristic manner when it was put to her that it was more or less obligatory for any visitor to the city to go up the Eiffel Tower.

'In that case,' said Hannah, a hint of steel glistening through that legendary sweetness, 'perhaps I should not have bothered to come to Paris.'

On the way to the Eiffel Tower.

When the appointed time for the proposed ascent arrived on a bitterly cold morning, Hannah climbed out of her taxi and looked up at the giant structure – the first close-up of Gustave Eiffel's great monument is always awe-inspiring. Her companions stood around in total silence, camera and sound recording equipment at the ready, but fully expecting her to decline the offer of a bird's-eye view of Paris and walk away.

Hannah, tight-lipped and pale, said not one word as she digested for several, long moments the scope of the ordeal ahead and then, with purposeful stride, set off for the lift in the North Pier, pursued by a vastly relieved film crew.

I'll not pretend that I had any fancy to go up that enormous thing. I had been dreading the prospect and feared it would bring problems into my life since I knew what was expected of me. Certainly, I would never have dared to go up it on my own because I am not one for heights and I have a creepy feeling about edges and long drops. But when I got to the lift I found it was much more solid and enclosed than I had imagined and I was lucky to find a seat in the corner where I could hide myself away on the way up.

A challenge successfully met – a telescopic view from the top of the Eiffel Tower.

In the famous Café de la Paix.

But oh, how I enjoyed it when I got to the top – well, to the second level, which is 115 metres high and quite far enough for my taste. Going to the very top, another 200 metres further up, would have definitely been beyond me. It was a glorious view and I soon got over a certain wariness about going right up to the railings. I am so glad I overcame my nerves – it would have been a dreadful shame to miss such an experience – and after a bit I grew quite confident, and walked about all around it. I would have stayed longer than I did but it was so cold up there – twice as cold as on the ground, even – that no one, not even the young and hardy could stand it for more than a few minutes. Ten at the most.

So I was glad to go and get warm again in the nicest of surroundings, the Café de la Paix, which is said to be the most famous pavement café in the whole of Paris. They also say that if you sit there long enough you will see every famous person in Europe pass by eventually, because it is just a few yards away from the Opera House. I certainly saw some interesting charac-

ters, extravagant even, when I took my coffee and cake. Such a variety of dress. But I expected to see more dogs in Paris – I thought the French were supposed to be as daft about dogs as me.

I got into conversation with a nice German couple sitting at the next table, and it turned out that they were from Heidelberg, one of the places on my European list. The gentleman told me that he preferred more open spaces to cities, so I recommended that he ought to visit our north country, particularly Teesdale, should he ever come to Britain.

Then came the biggest thrill of all, as far as my Paris trip was concerned. I walked a few yards from the Café de la Paix to the one place of all that I very badly wanted to see – the Paris Opéra. It symbolizes so much to a person like me who has been sustained all through life by music, something instilled in me by my mother, who was an accomplished musician. My dream of dreams would have been to become a professional musician, but that was just not possible. So when I entered that wonderful place I was very thrilled and very moved to think of all the great stars who had performed there down the years, and all the famous personalities, such as royalty and world statesmen, who had gone there to hear them. I could almost feel their presence.

It was an overwhelming place, with sweeping marble staircases, enormous chandeliers and mirrors, and beautifully fashioned carvings and painted ceilings. And my visit there ended with a rather wonderful and curious incident. I wasn't aware of it, but apparently the place closed whilst I was wandering around. They had missed me when they had ushered out the rest of the public and I found myself alone, except for Mostafa Hammuri, who was taking still pictures of me, since he was unable to use his film camera. A lady came towards us after a while – obviously one of the Opéra officials – but she said nothing and just watched me moving about, absorbing all the beauty of it. And then she approached and asked if I would like to see the auditorium, which was locked. I said I would be eternally grateful so she produced a key and opened up one of the boxes.

A very special place – the Paris Opera House.

And would you believe . . . they were beginning a rehearsal of the ballet, *Giselle*. She allowed me to watch for a while and that

Small person, large steps – at the Trocadero.

capped it all. A box at the Opéra – what a privilege. The experience will always have a special place in my memory.

Later on Mostafa told me that the kind lady had been under the impression that I was his aunt, and that she told him she thought I was a lovely lady with a very photogenic face and that he must be a very fond nephew!

As it happens, he is only ten years younger than me! But I didn't mind a bit – just look where it got me!

2

Down the Rhine With My Friend Frau Schneider

The second stage of Miss Hannah's travels diverted for a few days from the footsteps of Miss Jemima Morrell, and picked up the trail of a quartet of other daring ladies, the Misses Libbie, Hattie, Lucilla and Marian Lincolne, all daughters of a Norfolk gentleman of note. After long deliberation, they decided upon a cruise down the Rhine, a high priority for the Victorian middle classes, for their first venture to foreign parts – long before the turn of the century. They went with Mr Thomas Cook, and, true to form, they kept a meticulous journal:

The Lincolne sisters – a formidable-looking foursome.

*'Tis true we encountered some opposition . . . one friend
declaring it was improper for ladies to go alone. But one
interview with Mr Cook removed all our hesitation and we
forthwith placed ourselves under his care.*

*And how well we remember the happy group we formed as
we sat on the paddle box of the steamer, commanding a
view of both sides of the beautiful Rhine.*

One has to admire the enterprise of the Misses Lincolne for refusing to conform to those stifling Victorian values. I think I would have felt the same way had I lived in those times because I don't like to be made to conform either. Their example must have made it easier for others similarly placed, to break free and cross the Channel. It was all made much easier for me, of course. First there was a comfortable, if somewhat long rail journey from Paris to Cologne, where I stayed for just one night in the Dom Hotel, which like the George V is owned by the British hoteliers, Trusthouse Forte. It is situated in the giant shadow cast by Cologne Cathedral, which must be one of the tallest in the world. I had to crane my neck to see to the top of the spires, even from my bedroom window which was directly facing.

The British theme was carried on by the boat, since it had the good name *Britannia* and had murals featuring Nelson and Lady Hamilton, and a fox-hunting scene. It was called a Connoisseur Cruise and run by the KD Rhine Line, so I imagine it was their very best boat. Nicely furnished it was, too, and decidedly spacious. I had a magnificent suite on the main deck so I could see everything as we passed by. The boat even had a little swimming pool but the weather continued to be poor, so I never saw anyone use it. They kept it heated just in case, and it made a sad sight, steam rising from the surface and totally neglected.

It is a great broad river, the Rhine, and very busy, too, with commercial traffic, but what we all came to see of course were the castles. I never expected there to be so many. Some of them seemed to be perched very precariously on the hilltops and I wondered how they managed to stop from tumbling down.

Even though I expect they were stoutly built, I wouldn't have liked to live in one myself.

> *What masses of rock and cascades of water. What fertility.*
> *How many such spots of loveliness are there on the earth.*

EXTRACT FROM THE JOURNAL OF THE MISSES LINCOLNE

There certainly were some very steep places and nice waterfalls along the Rhine and many of them had acres and acres of vines growing down the slopes. I wondered how on earth the farmers stayed on their feet, never mind managing to plant and harvest the grapes. And I am not sure I can entirely agree with the Misses Lincolnes' sentiments about the loveliness of the scenery.

The Good Ship *Britannia.*

Miss Loreley, posing on top of the legendary rock.

But I expect the sun was shining when they travelled along the Rhine. Fine weather makes all the difference to the looks of any place.

> *We saw the enormous rock of Loreley and we could distinctly see a face in the outline of the rock. Eyelashes and every feature were perfect.*

EXTRACT FROM THE JOURNAL OF THE MISSES LINCOLNE

We hadn't been going along very long when we, too, passed the Loreley Rock where legend says the lady with long golden hair used to lure sailors to their deaths, and people come from all over the world to see it. I understand that a young local lady with similar looks who was the current Miss Loreley was waving to our boat from the very top, but it was too far for me to spot her. I even missed seeing the famous statue on the bank, so I saw much less of the Loreley than the Misses Lincolne!

But I did get to meet another lovely young girl when we stopped for the night at Rüdesheim, and I was taken in a vintage car to a rather interesting hotel where the local Wine Queen was waiting to greet me with an enormous glass of wine – they said it held an entire bottle. I was pleased to be told it was non-alcoholic, so I had a sip. The hotel was very old and called the Lindenwirt, and built in a sort of Elizabethan half-timbered style. But it turned out to be of modern construction, partly at least. The proprietor told me it had been badly damaged by bombs during the last war. When his father returned home from serving in the army he brought back with him a comrade, who couldn't go back to his own home because it was in the East, and he turned out to be a skilled craftsman. They set about restoring the hotel to its original state, even going out into the forest to chop down oak trees because wood was so scarce at the time.

I had another grand night, eating and being serenaded by a nice man with a piano accordion, who funnily enough reminded me strongly of a man I used to know back in Teesdale, called George Robinson. Towards the end there was another quite wonderful episode – they did seem to happen regularly on my

Dinner at Rüdesheim with Annamarie van Assendelft of the local tourist office.

travels – when a gentleman came across and presented me with a red rose. Someone explained that he was a senior official of the new Romanian government on a visit to the Rhine. A translator explained that he wished to extend a cordial invitation to visit his country as his guest. Apparently, the interpreter was married to an English girl, who had read the books and seen the programmes and he had recognized me and explained who I was. He said that an official invitation would follow by post but I don't know what I'll do about it if and when it does arrive.

But the thing which really galvanized Hannah's trip down the Rhine, from Cologne to Basle, was the Frau Schneider factor. Lisa Schneider is an irrepressible eighty-one-year-old widow who travels the Rhine on KD Cruises two or three times a year. She is well known to all the *Britannia* crew, from the Captain down to the man who swabs the decks. She danced, sang and bounced around the boat from dawn until the last glass of champagne had been

A dance with Ann, our assistant cameraperson.

43

quaffed (it was even offered with breakfast) and wore an amazing selection of dramatic clothes, predominantly gold and silver lamé, which she rotated several times a day. She homed in on Hannah at the Captain's reception on the first night, and they became inseparable. Neither knew more than three words of each other's language, but they chatted for hours on end!

Party night on the Rhine, with Lisa Schneider on the left.

Oh, yes, lovely Lisa, she became such a good friend. I first saw her at the entrance to the reception and she smiled and gave a little bow, then came over to sit with me. There was a language problem, of course, but we managed to brush along with smiles and gestures and good will, and because we liked each other so much. Mostly, I hadn't a clue what she was saying and I only hope I said 'Yes' and 'No' in the right places. It was hard to believe she was an octogenarian because she had twice as much go in her than me.

I found out a little of Lisa's background from the odd occasions we were in conversation with someone who understood both English and German, and I would have liked to have learned more – but not in a nosy way, you understand. She told me she had lost her husband five years previously and lived in Düsseldorf. I also gathered that there was some family connection in Argentina, and at first I thought she had a grandson, because she showed me a lovely little suit for a boy she had just bought. But it turned out to be for the son of one of the men working on the boat. Apparently, she knew all the crew very well because she was such a regular passenger.

I did manage to put together the details of one story she was trying to tell me, about being in Berlin at the outbreak of the last war, and how she set off to try and join her brother – and a sister – or it could have been two sisters - in Argentina. But then she

A toast from my friend, Lisa.

met a gentleman on the way and married him. Where their journey ended I never found out, but she was married to the man for forty-five years.

Lisa was always ready for a bit of fun – she drank five glasses of champagne at the Captain's farewell reception – and one night after a splendid dinner on board she grabbed my stick and started a very energetic dance routine, which amused everyone. She was so good at it that I wondered whether or not she had been a stage artist at some time in her life.

But for all her jollity I think there must have been a sad side to Lisa. I would hazard a guess that she was a lonely lady. And rather well off, I fancy, judging by her clothes and the money she spent on gifts. She even bought jewellery for me – there was just no stopping her.

I was most grateful for her company, and she escorted me round the city of Strasbourg when the boat docked there for a day and by dint of sign language I gathered that she had lived there for a while when she was a child. Another day we went to-

A cup of tea in Strasbourg.

With Lisa in
Strasbourg.

In front of Strasbourg's
magnificent Cathedral.

gether on a coach trip to Heidelberg. Now there's a grand place, very medieval, and built in a very nice red stone all along the banks of the river and dominated by the castle, which had been knocked about a bit by various wars down the centuries.

With Lisa, on the coach to Heidelberg.

I came across a rather strange coincidence in Heidelberg. Our guide told us that Mark Twain had spent a lot of time there, and had written his book *Innocents Abroad* whilst living in a house perched on one of the big hills surrounding the city.

There were a lot of trees on those hills and the various shades of green and bronze were very unusual, and a treat for the eyes – almost as though an artist had painted them. I always look for the greenery around, more so than the buildings, however splendid and historic they may be. And I noticed a big difference between our own English trees and those I saw in both France and Germany. At home we have lots of trees with big thick trunks, many too large to put your two arms around. But on the Continent they all seem to be very slender, even in the Bois de Boulogne in Paris. I wonder what the explanation can be.

In the shopping area of
Heidelberg.

In the gardens of
Heidelberg Castle,
with Lisa.

I also noticed another difference – between the overall character of the French and the Germans. Apart from Lisa of course, the Germans seemed to be a touch stiff and formal. They are most efficient and correct but you don't usually break any ice with them. They seem to smile in a professional kind of way, if you get my meaning, whereas the French are more Latin in temperament and show their feelings rather more. Not that I have anything against the Germans because they were most courteous towards me, particularly the ladies who helped to run the boat.

The view from Heidelberg Castle.

There was a tearful scene when the cruise ended for Hannah in Basle and she and Frau Lisa Schneider, who was staying with the boat all the way to Amsterdam, had to part. It was a long farewell, marked by the exchange of gifts, addresses, and many promises to write and to try and meet again somewhere, sometime. And the whirlwind lady from Düsseldorf had fallen completely under the curious spell that Hannah casts over people – Lisa and a dozen

A sad farewell to Lisa.

other people on the boat had watched in tears when a video tape of 'A Winter Too Many', the most recent Yorkshire Television documentary about the life of the lady from Low Birk Hatt, was shown on a television in the bar one night.

It is an even bet that one day Frau Lisa Schneider, will join the steady stream of pilgrims who make their way to Belle Vue Cottage, Cotherstone.

3

The Alpine Experience –
and Another Challenge

*Crossing the threshold of Switzerland we entered on a line
of scenery that bewildered us by its beauty . . . Frowning
mountains reflected in shimmering lakes . . . while an
atmosphere of delicious sweetness hung in the valleys.*

*Oh that the retina could be enamelled with the grandeur of
that matchless landscape.*

EXTRACT FROM MISS JEMIMA MORRELL'S JOURNAL

Miss Jemima Morrell was clearly quite overcome by her first
glimpse of the Alps when she travelled there under the personal
supervision of Mr Thomas Cook in 1863. Not so Miss Hannah Hauxwell. When, a century and a half later, she picked up her predecessor's path again after the cruise down the Rhine, her reaction
to the glories of the Alps was in sharp contrast. And when the time
came to board the mountain railway train which grinds its way up
steeply from Chamonix to the Mer de Glace, a flowing mass of ice
nearly six thousand feet above sea level, she was almost as nervous
as the occasion when she faced up to the challenge of the Eiffel
Tower.

Given the choice I certainly wouldn't have
followed in Miss Jemima's footsteps at this point of her tour. I
didn't really like it at all. That train worried me, going straight up
the mountain like it did. I know it's an outstanding feat of
engineering, but I was rather concerned to discover that there
was only one driver. I mean, we are all human, and what if he
had had a heart attack on the way. No, I like my own two feet on
the ground, not up in the skies like that. I'm just not good with
heights, and the mountains seem to be so close and forbidding. I
much prefer the hills of Baldersdale.

It was a bit better when we got to the top and there was a little
more elbow room, but I'm afraid the Mer de Glace didn't do a lot
for me. I know it's magnificent in its own way and millions travel
to see it, but I fell out with snow and ice years ago. It was all right
when I was young, when a heavy snowfall meant I didn't have
to go to school, but my enthusiasm dwindled down the years
when I had to cut a way through every winter to find the

A reluctant passenger –
the mountain train
from Chamonix.

The crevices in the Mer de Glace.

Overlooking the Mer de Glace.

Taking tea
on the roof
of Europe.

water for the cattle. If I never saw snow again as long as I lived I wouldn't mind at all.

Now, I was grateful to experience the Mer de Glace, even though it wasn't my kind of beauty, and I can appreciate why people such as Miss Jemima, who probably never had to battle with snow to keep beasties alive, were greatly impressed. She even went down the path that leads from the viewing platform down to the ice crevasses below, which looked very deep and dangerous to me.

> *How strange, how intensely incongruous it felt on that hot*
> *summer's day, to be crunching ice under our feet, and to*
> *be looking down yawning crevasses that showed eighty or*
> *a hundred feet of their blue and crystal lined jaws.*

EXTRACT FROM MISS JEMIMA MORRELL'S JOURNAL

Now that was a pleasure I was happy to forego. All credit to Miss Jemima, but I think she was a good bit younger than me at the time and certainly a lot more adventurous. Only if the train had toppled over and there was no other way back would I have gone down there.

Neither did I care much for Chamonix, the place we set off from. It is situated right at the foot of Mont Blanc which I understand is the biggest mountain in Europe, and Miss Jemima wrote that she couldn't take her eyes off it, she was so entranced. But it's so high and so near to the town that it gave me an enclosed, restricted feeling – is the word claustrophobic? I certainly couldn't live in Chamonix.

The Mer de Glace.

Tea and fancies on the hotel balcony in Geneva.

I much preferred Geneva, largely because of the water, since a lake always reminds me of the reservoir just below Low Birk Hatt. And the snow was quite a distance away, just visible on top of the mountains. I stayed there before moving into the Alps, at the Hotel des Berges, where Miss Jemima also lodged. I was just as impressed by the place as she was, and apparently some magazine has named it one of the best thirty hotels in the world. I was served tea and little fancy cakes on a balcony overlooking Lake Leman, with a good view of the enormous fountain which I understand is the best known feature of Geneva. It must shoot a hundred feet in the air, and someone said it was the best shower in the world, if you could only stand the cold!

There were everlasting hills on the road from Geneva to Chamonix. It was a relief occasionally to see a little bit of green and a farmstead now and again. And there were such a lot of houses in some areas. At times it seemed like an epidemic of houses, almost like a shanty town, because they appeared to be quite insubstantial, particularly the roofs. Not at all like our own stone-built dwellings. And then there must be the threat of the snow coming down from the hills and landing right on the top of them.

Towards the end of the journey the motorway rose up on stilts to a fair height and I was a bit quakey about that, too.

Caution should have been my middle name, you know!

My impression of Chamonix improved a little – but only a little – when we rested there for a day after the ordeal of the mountain railway to the Mer de Glace. It was a Sunday and it rained steadily from dawn until nightfall. The mountains were hidden behind mist and low cloud, but the air was full of the music of church bells, which I enjoyed. Then from my bedroom window I watched a band marching round the streets, leading a procession of firemen in their shiny brass helmets, policemen in those

One of the dramatic statues, left, and me, right, in the centre of Chamonix.

very striking hats like General de Gaulle always used to wear on ceremonial occasions and what I took to be local dignitaries dressed in their best clothes. Very few carried umbrellas, certainly none of the fire and police officers, and they just marched bravely on obviously soaked to the skin. I didn't find out what the occasion was but it was obviously important to them.

There are two very striking statues in the centre of Chamonix, close by the river, which is an unusual mint-green colour and rushes through the valley at an alarming speed. They were romantic representations of the men who first conquered Mont Blanc way back in the eighteenth century, and I noticed particularly that one looked uncannily like Michael Heseltine. Now I concede that they must have been very courageous men, but personally I cannot understand why people want to climb such places and risk life and limb. I appreciate the challenge it represents but it's such a shame when young men get cut off in the prime of life, as they so often do climbing those fearsome heights.

The next stage of my journey took me back across the border into Switzerland, following Miss Jemima to another place which thrilled her to bits, called Saint Martin. The drive through the valleys was a truly enjoyable experience, but Saint Martin turned out to be a tiny village situated high up in the mountains, and the road to it was frightening. It wasn't very wide and some of the edges weren't protected very well at all, so you wouldn't have had a hope if something had gone wrong. I saw sheer drops of some hundreds of feet. And Miss Jemima must have travelled the same way when things were far less comfortable – by horse-drawn carriage, I imagine, which was very brave of her. I would not have liked to have entrusted my safety on that road to some flighty horses.

Apparently, she was very anxious to get to Saint Martin because she had been assured that the view from there alone was worth the trip from London. Well, I am glad she liked it so much, because it would have been a great pity not to have, after all the time, trouble and risks she had endured to reach it. But I am afraid, with all due respect to an enterprising lady, that I could not agree. I much prefer the trees and the fields in the valleys on the way to Saint Martin with the mountains at a re-

spectable distance. Up there I was reminded of the old saying that he that is low may fear no fall. It was cold, too, a real windy ridge of a place, and I was amazed at the position of some of the little houses, which seemed to be perched very precariously on the edge of steep drops. There must be no shelter in winter – one wonders how they manage, those who choose to live in such places.

After Saint Martin I went on an even worse road, twisting and turning and clinging to the hillsides, up to a place called Leukerbad, where they have some very famous thermal baths. It is situated in a hollow with steep mountains rising all around it, and I was somewhat disturbed to learn it had been destroyed several times by avalanches with much loss of life. But that had been a long time ago and the town had since been protected by a series of barriers, which I could see from my hotel room. Leukerbad seemed to be much nearer the sky than Chamonix, so there wasn't the same oppressive feel to it. As for the thermal baths, I approached them with some reluctance because there was a cold wind blowing from the mountains which went clean through the long striped bathing robe they loaned me. But I did enjoy the

In hot water in Leukerbad.

On the way to St Martin, left.

warmth when I finally made it down the steps, although I didn't move around once I was immersed because there seemed to be a strong current, which created a lot of bubbles, and I don't swim.

The best part of Leukerbad was the music man in the hotel who was very skilful with the piano accordion, playing some jolly pieces. He was a recording artist, too, and I acquired some of his tapes.

Later on I heard a very different kind of instrument which had obviously pleased Miss Jemima – the alpenhorn.

The notes died away in softest cadence, which notes were taken up by the mountains and reverberated by them again and again.

EXTRACT FROM THE JOURNAL OF MISS JEMIMA MORRELL

A lady in traditional Swiss dress played for me at the top of the Semmental valley and I am sorry to say I had to beg to differ with Miss Jemima once again. The alpenhorn looks like a great long

The alpenhorn – pretty sight, not so pretty sound!

smoking pipe, light in colour and nicely decorated at the end. It's an instrument that might be nice with an orchestra but as a solo instrument I wouldn't go many yards to hear it, really. It made a doleful sound that reminded me of the old Dales' saying that 'it sounds like the tune an old cow makes when it's dying'.

Then I was taken to see a herd of those pretty Swiss cows which make their own kind of music from the bells round their necks. They were a strange breed to me, white and light ginger like the old kind of Ayrshires used to be, and the farmer told me they were a mixture of Holstein and Semmental. They seemed to be much like a variety of Friesian to my reckoning. Not my kind of beasts really, although they were very quiet and manageable, even the little ones. No, there was nothing much to remind me of my own herd – in the days, not long ago, when I had one. My family I used to call them. I still own Rosa, of course, who is looked after by a good friend, and I didn't see one in that Swiss herd to compare with her.

Making friends with a beastie and her owner.

It was fair to say that Hannah was singularly unimpressed with the majesty of Switzerland. Indeed, she confirmed this beyond doubt when she was taken to a point high above Interlaken in the Bernese Oberland to view the range which includes the Eiger and the Jungfrau. The day was glorious, the view breathtaking, although the summits of those two magnificent peaks were obscured by cloud . . . at first. Hannah thoroughly enjoyed this inspirational vista, but her observations at the time made it perfectly clear that she was always looking down, not up.

Oh yes, I like this. The hills covered with trees, and the water of two lakes on either side of Interlaken reflecting the blue sky. Any place with water is special to me, having lived alongside water for most of my life. And down there it's like a carpet with all the different shades of green and the tiny houses . . .

An unusual water trough near Lenk.

The lakes at Interlaken, right.

Quite suddenly and dramatically in the middle of this interview the sun burned off the top mists and the peaks of the Eiger and Jung-frau appeared. The effect on the group alongside Hannah was electric. She was urged to look up and give her impression. And in a small, reluctant, indifferent voice she murmured: 'Oh . . . er . . . quite magnificent.'

It was a classic example of something being damned with faint praise, or as Miss Dorothy Parker once put it, being praised with a faint damn!

Interlaken – the Eiger and Jungfrau in the background.

4

Austria, the Land of Music ... and My Meetings With Mr Mozart and Mr Strauss

The first thing I noticed – with some relief – about Austria when I entered it from Switzerland was that the hills were further away with a lot of level land in between. Please don't imagine that I wasn't grateful to have the privilege of visiting Switzerland, but it is not a place I would choose to visit again. It's just that I like to have a bit of space around me, so Austria turned out to be more suited to my tastes.

I arrived in Salzburg under a rain-cloud which must have followed me all the way from Interlaken, and it never stopped for two days. But that didn't prevent me from appreciating the beauty of the city, which was more my size – easy to come to grips with – and very old and elegant. They call it the Rome north of the Alps, since it has more Italian influence than German. I was told that it rains there on average two hundred days a year, and I didn't get a glimpse of the surrounding hills until the day I left. It is obviously a very religious city with 120 places of worship for a population of 145,000, and there are ten different monastic orders, which appear to own much of the property around.

View from the hill overlooking Salzburg.

In Mozart Square,
Salzburg, with Mr
Mozart in the
background.

But the soul of Austria is its music, and Salzburg appears to be dedicated to the memory of its most famous son, Wolfgang Amadeus Mozart. I understood that for a whole year there was to be a Mozart concert every evening somewhere in the city, because they were commemorating the two-hundredth anniversary of his death. The Mozart statue is to be found in Mozart Square and there are even Mozart chocolates in the shops! The Austrians, however, did not appreciate him very much during his lifetime since he ended up in a pauper's grave.

I like some of his music, but there's a lot I don't know much about. He was probably a genius but the flame which burned so brightly soon flickered away and died, sadly. But someone did once say that maybe it's better to be remembered for great achievements than to deteriorate in later life into a shadow of one's former self.

Hannah attended a concert in the magnificent marble hall of the Mirabell Palace in Salzburg, and the occasion was altogether reminiscent of the ballroom scene from Cinderella. Resplendent in a long, purple ball gown, Hannah ascended a flight of polished stone stairs dripping with statuary and lanterns and moved very carefully into a seat under an enormous crystal chandelier, close by a glistening white grand piano. Her filmed arrival caused a ripple of interest and it later transpired that the audience had generally supposed that she was the tutor of the eminent pianist due to play that night.

It was a lovely experience, of course, and I did have that Cinderella feeling, but the odd thing was that it must have been one of the few concerts heard in Salzburg that year which didn't have any music by Mozart! The programme, for solo piano, included pieces by César Franck, Stravinsky and Franz Liszt. I par-

The Mirabell Palace in Salzburg.
Austrian National Tourist Office

ticularly enjoyed the Liszt. The concert hall was wonderful and very high, which I imagine helped the acoustics, and the artist was a Mr David Lively, a young American gentleman, and he was very skilful. He had no sheet music, so he played difficult pieces entirely from memory, which was very impressive.

I met another American in Salzburg, who guided me around the place and she turned out to be a Miss Dale Ellen Shumanski. Now we had no footsteps of Victorian maiden ladies to follow in Salzburg – I am sure they did visit, but no journals could be traced – so there I was being led by a twentieth-century maiden lady, which I thought was very appropriate. She had come to Salzburg to study more than twenty years ago and liked the area so much she stayed on. And like me, she was the daughter of a farmer. She had been born and raised on a farm in New York State, so we had much in common. And she was an author, too, and presented me with her book, all about the von Trapp family and the making of the film, *The Sound of Music*, which was shot in and around Salzburg. She had even met Julie Andrews.

And there was another coincidence concerning the family who ran the hotel I stayed in, which was more like a country house, since it was situated in a large garden with little lakes, on the outskirts of Salzburg. They were called Schneider, which, of course, brought back the memories of the good times on the Rhine with Lisa Schneider, and made me wonder how her voyage to Amsterdam had gone.

They had a dog called Tommy, which was a mix of Irish setter and alsatian, which I wanted to take for a walk in the gardens. But it turned out to be very fierce, a real guard dog, so I was obliged to avoid it, and I ended by being accompanied by the granddaughter of the senior Mr Schneider, who owned Tommy.

I became better acquainted with a couple of horses which pulled the carriage I rode in around the centre of Salzburg. They caused me quite a bit of concern because it was raining so hard and they had no protection whatsoever. The drivers were well wrapped up, and I think they could have done something for their horses, which had to do a lot of standing about. It was cold, as well. One of them was quite frisky and pawed the ground when it was anxious to set off, or getting bored. He reminded me of a horse I once owned called Prince, which had the same habit.

The ride was fascinating despite the weather and I saw all the old buildings, fountains, statues and archways. And some beautiful ornamental gardens.

A damp horse and carriage ride in Salzburg.

One morning Miss Dale Ellen took me to a very odd place, the Hellbrunn Palace, which had been built as a hunting lodge in the seventeenth century by one of the Prince Archbishops who ruled the area in those days. He obviously had a strange sense of humour because he installed a vast number of trick fountains.

For instance, he had built a large stone table with seven seats for drinking parties in the garden. It had a well in the centre to cool the wine and, apparently, when the party was in full swing he would give a signal and water would shoot up from all the seats but his. And because it was not permitted for anyone to rise before the Prince Archbishop they had to grin and bear it. We watched it being demonstrated – and it was a marvellous thing to realize that it had been working for nearly four centuries – but I would not have liked to have been one of his guests.

There were many other unpleasant surprises in that place.

Hidden jets set off unexpectedly all over the place, and even the antlers of carved deer-heads suddenly spouted water. I watched a large party of tourists being guided round the castle, and a lot of them got very wet. As though we hadn't seen enough of water in Salzburg! To me it wasn't funny, to be drenched like that on a cold day, and I didn't form a good opinion of the Prince Archbishop. Maybe I'm an old stick-in-the-mud but I think practical jokers are a pain in the neck. I just think it was a pity that such a splendid place had been built with people's discomfort in mind.

The next step on my Grand Tour was the city which ranks second to Paris in my affections, Vienna. For me it is the city of Johann Strauss. I know that Vienna has strong associations with other famous composers, such as Beethoven, Haydn, Schubert and Brahms, but Strauss has a special place in my heart. I'll never forget seeing the film about him, called *The Great Waltz*. Even if the day is dull and sad, just listening to Johann Strauss

The Hellbrunn Palace in Salzburg.
Austrian National Tourist Office

A meeting with my hero, Johann Strauss, in Vienna.

The Vienna Woods.
Austrian National Tourist Office

transports me into other worlds. It always makes me think of beautiful places. I know some people say his music is light and frothy, which I do not think is justified. Take the 'Emperor' Waltz, for instance . . . it has some marvellous chords, some very solemn. He has the ability to tell a sad story for a while, and then it blossoms out into life and beauty. They were a unique family, the Strausses. There was the senior Johann, and it was a pity he became estranged from his son in the end, and then the brother Joseph, who wrote 'Roses from the South', which I like very much. But Johann Strauss II is the number one for me. I spent some time admiring the extremely romantic statue of him in the garden of the park in the centre of Vienna which is quite unlike the rather sombre figures one usually sees. Johann is playing his violin, surrounded by a kind of marble halo which is carved into representations of lovers, with one couple at the top kissing each other. Very appropriate, since his music has inspired romantic love down the centuries.

I went to see the Danube, of course, and I had already been told not to expect it to be blue. But it did its best, and the sun came out for a while when I came to it. The colour was a kind of jade green that day, so I wasn't really disappointed. And I reminded myself that it had moved Johann to write one of his best-known and loved pieces, the 'Blue Danube' Waltz.

I was also pleased to see some nice dogs being taken for a walk along the banks of the Danube, including an English setter and even a little Yorkshire terrier! There seemed to be more dogs around in Austria, particularly when compared with France and Switzerland.

Then I was taken on a tour of the city, by a friend of a friend who has a lovely flat in the old part. She was called Maria Dietrich – *Miss* Dietrich, would you believe! She told me when she was much younger – during the time when Marlene Dietrich was famous throughout the world, especially for her beautiful legs – she used to cause a stir whenever she presented her passport on crossing a border because it was made out simply to M. Dietrich. Apparently, the immigration people would invariably get up to examine her legs!

Vienna is much bigger than Salzburg and you had to go looking for the sights, whereas in Mozart's city they were all in one

place. I badly wanted to see the Opera House, which ranks second to the Paris Opéra, I believe, so Maria guided me there and told me how the music lovers of Vienna would queue all night for tickets if someone like Placido Domingo was appearing. And I saw St Stephen's Cathedral with its mosaic roof, the very centre and oldest part of Vienna. Maria said that most of the area had been badly damaged during the last war, including that famous roof. But the steeple had been miraculously spared. The city is dotted with very impressive churches and public buildings, mostly built in the nineteenth century, and I appreciated them all.

According to Maria, Vienna had a very rough time of it during the war, and many important buildings and homes were destroyed. She was fortunate to be living in southern Austria at the time, but very nearly ended up behind the Russian lines. It seems the fleeing German army stopped just a mile or two away from her town and held the line, so her home ended up in the British sector when the country was divided like Germany. She

The Vienna skyline, with St Stephen's Cathedral.
Austrian National Tourist Office

Vienna's Opera House.
*Austrian National
Tourist Office*

The dreaded Prater Wheel in Vienna.

was fourteen at the time and described a very difficult situation. She said that food was in very short supply. Curiously, the experience created a habit which is very strong in me – an inability to throw anything away, particularly food. Like me, she usually takes away for future use any leftovers from the restaurant table.

I liked Vienna and enjoyed every moment, save for the occasion when I followed in the footsteps of Harry Lime and rode on the Prater, the giant ferris wheel which is so well remembered from the film, *The Third Man*. I hated going up and over the top at such a great height – indeed, I felt more secure going up the Eiffel Tower. No, Harry Lime is welcome to that thing.

But to more than compensate for that, my Viennese experience ended on the highest of notes in more ways than one. On the last night I was taken up the hills on the outskirts of the city where the famous Vienna woods are situated. The ground not taken up by trees is covered with vineyards – more than a thousand acres of them. The streets on the way up to the hills are dotted with dozens of wine taverns called *heurigers*, which all have a sprig of pine hung up over the door. They are busy, noisy but happy places with wooden booths and lots of plump, blond,

The house where Beethoven once lived.

A marvellous, musical night at the wine cellar in Vienna.

waitresses bustling around serving the wine and food. I went to a famous one near the house where Beethoven once lived and had a marvellous meal, with lots of tender meat and some rather tasty dumplings. Fortunately, they served soft drinks as well as wine.

Better than all of that was the music – live music! Three musicians came in and began to play all my favourite Strauss melodies. There was a mandolin player, a piano-accordionist and, best of all, a violinist. The gentleman with the mandolin also sang, and came to serenade me. Just me!

And the evening ended with a gentleman presenting me with a lovely long-stemmed red rose.

Yes, I will go back to Vienna any time!

5

Goodnight Vienna, Good Morning Italy … and the Forty-Seven Tunnels to Florence

Hannah's Viennese experience appreciably revived her spirits and she was much taken by the sights encountered on the long drive to Florence. The fear that the strain of foreign travel, plus the pressures of filming, would grind the enterprise to a halt were beginning to recede. There was a time in Vienna when the situation hung in the balance for several hours when Hannah had what she called one of her 'funny turns', and was obliged to take to her bed. The agonizing point about that incident was that it coincided with the first really fine weather of the entire trip – but it only lasted while Hannah was indisposed. That the YTV crew was able to sunbathe in the Vienna hills for the entire morning was scarcely a redeeming feature. But much reassurance was afforded by the appetite of the lady. Pound for pound she was ingesting as many, if not more calories than anyone else, and clearly enjoyed every mouthful. And she derived much entertainment from the numerous short tunnels through the mountains after the Italian border was negotiated, and counted them all with an innocent glee.

The Duomo in Udine.
Italian State Tourist Office

Yes, there were forty-seven altogether. Twenty-five on the way to Udine, a very nice place where we stayed the night, and another twenty-two from there to Florence. I thought it much like speeding through the lens of a camera. Suddenly you would come out of the darkness and see a lovely view for just a few seconds – wooded hills, snow-capped peaks, valleys with a farmstead dotted here and there – and then back into darkness again. Every vista was different and fascinating in its own way. Those tunnels certainly shortened the journey for me.

But there was a problem when we finally arrived in Florence. By this time we were following the path of another maiden lady who had travelled with Mr Thomas Cook over a century ago, a Miss M. J. Furby of Bridlington in Yorkshire. Her journal was a mite more understated than that of Miss Jemima Morrell who went into such rhapsodies over Switzerland.

> *We arrived in Florence on Sunday afternoon and took a carriage to the hill of San Miniato, where we obtained a magnificent view of the city and environs of Florence, and the windings of the River Arno.*
>
> EXTRACT FROM THE JOURNAL OF MISS M. J. FURBY

Well, I travelled immediately to this very same spot, but I had to wear a thick sweater and protect myself with an umbrella. The weather was dreadful, all grey skies and rain which was made worse by the news that Britain was enjoying sun and clear skies. All I could see from that elevated view was a mass of very wet red roofs and a decidedly murky river. As someone said at the time, it looked a bit like Barnsley!

> *And then we saw Michelangelo's David, eighteen feet high.*
>
> EXTRACT FROM THE JOURNAL OF MISS M. J. FURBY

Yes, I took a good look at that too, which was on the same hill in the Piazza Michelangelo. Now it's a fine statue in a fine square, but it's just a replica, after all. Michelangelo didn't chisel it himself. It's not the real quill, as we used to say in Baldersdale. And

The best view of Florence and the river Arno – when it isn't raining! In the centre of Florence, Neptune in the background, right. The Piazza Michelangelo with a replica of David.
Italian State Tourist Office

it had been cast in bronze and turned into an unattractive green colour. Also, it was upsetting to see all the graffiti around the bottom of the plinth – I wonder why people do such a thing.

The elements were unbelievably cruel during Hannah's stay in Florence. Heavy rain was followed by a violent thunderstorm, which emptied the streets of tourists, provided the purveyors of plastic macs and umbrellas with a bonanza and finally pounded the city with hailstones large enough to stun the pigeons. The region's newspapers recorded the chilling fact that it was the coldest and wettest start to the Tuscan summer since 1930! In between the downpours there was one brief hour of sunshine and Hannah hurried down to the Piazza close to the Uffizi Gallery where she viewed the equestrian statue of the first Medici to rule Tuscany, the giant statue of Neptune and the other, much photographed replica of Michelangelo's David.

Well, I much preferred that version because it was in real stone, marble I would imagine. It made all the difference. The other figures in the square were splendid sights too. The sunshine helped, of course, and the visit was made even brighter when a lady and gentleman came up to me when I was admiring David and introduced themselves. They had seen my television programmes and read the books, too. They lived near Ullswater in the Lake District and asked me all sorts of questions. Lovely people, and very British. They said they were intending to visit Cotherstone at some point in the future, and I will certainly make them very welcome if they do. It is remarkable how many people recognize me when I'm out and about.

Afterwards I walked down to the river Arno alongside the Uffizi Gallery, which is vast. There was such a long queue to enter the gallery it would have taken too much of my limited time in Florence to get in, but I didn't really mind because the city is one enormous art gallery. There are priceless sculptures round every corner and the cathedral, which I was told was the third longest in the world, must be the most colourful. All pink, green and white marble. It takes fifteen minutes to walk round the perimeter.

Then I decided that under no circumstances must I miss the

Florence's Ponte
Vecchio.
*Italian State Tourist
Office*

chance of acquiring a memento of Florence from the famous
Ponte Vecchio, the bridge over the river which is lined on both
sides by tiny jewellers' shops where they have been working
with precious metals and stones for centuries. It was a very busy
place, full of tourists jostling to buy – they were spending for-
tunes – and I had to wait for several minutes before there was
room for me to enter the shop I fancied. I particularly wanted a
cameo brooch and the shop specialized in them. The man
showed me the big pink shells they were worked from and after
much deliberation I made my selection. Since it had a dual purpose as either brooch or pendant the gentleman persuaded me
to buy an eighteen-carat gold chain as well, so I could wear it as a
necklace. He offered me discount if I paid cash, which caused all

89

A silver shop on the Ponte Vecchio.
Italian State Tourist Office

sorts of confusion because they give you over two thousand lire to the pound, which means their thousand lire note is only worth fifty pence, and the price of my two items came to 190,000 lire! There were notes flying all over the place as I dug for cash out of my purse. It made it seem much more extravagant, as indeed it was – almost a hundred pounds!

The same day I was taken to see some of Florence's most celebrated cloisters, in an ancient and beautiful children's hospital, which had a most poignant history. In times past the building had a large wheel arrangement connected to the street where unfortunate mothers, such as unmarried ladies, and those too poor to feed and clothe their infants, would place the child in the wheel and turn it round so that the little bundle would be deposited into care. That way the mother would remain anonymous, but I was told that many left a mark on their baby – I'm not sure just how – so they had positive proof if at some time in the future they were in a better position to support it. The practice had to stop in the 1870s when there was a near famine in the region and out of three thousand babies born in Florence one year, more

The Palace of Our Lady in Florence, right.
Italian State Tourist Office

than one thousand were pushed through that wheel. I have known difficult times myself, but it is impossible to comprehend the kind of poverty which drove mothers to that extreme. And I noticed that Italian parents are extremely loving and proud of their little ones, and dress them beautifully, particularly those pretty, dark-haired girls with such large brown eyes.

However, my visit to Florence ended on a happy note when I came across a room off one of the cloisters which is used for practice by music students. I listened for several pleasant moments as half a dozen young people played a very old Florentine-sounding piece on their wind instruments. One of them spoke good English and we had a chat after they had finished.

So . . . my path across Europe was consistently blessed by good music which made up in some measure for the unseasonable weather. I felt like the lady in the nursery rhyme who rode a white horse to Banbury Cross.

'She shall have music wherever she goes,' says the rhyme. And so it was for me.

6

My Road to Rome Via the Leaning Tower, With a Slight Argument in Siena

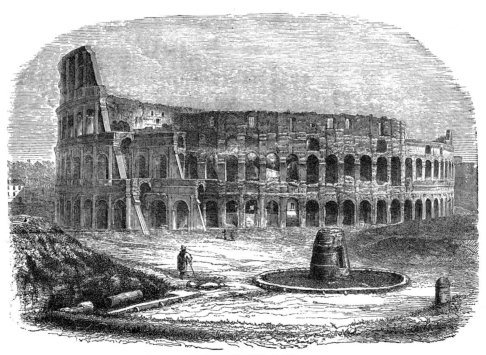

VIEW OF THE COLOSSEUM AT ROME.

All my summer dresses stayed in my case again as we proceeded southwards towards Rome and the forecasters' promise of fine weather proved unfounded. It was essential to go via Pisa, of course – it kept us on the trail of Miss Furby of Bridlington – and I found the place had much more to offer than just the leaning tower, which the locals must consider to be a miracle because the square in which it is situated is called the Piazza dei Miracoli. But I imagine that many tourists who only have eyes for the tower miss the fine area around the river Arno, which runs all the way from Florence to Pisa on its way to the sea. I noticed a magnificent display of roses and some splendid architecture.

Still, I was much impressed by the tower, just as Miss Furby was. She wrote about how a stone dropped from the top during her visit landed fifteen feet from the base. I imagine the distance would be much larger nowadays because it is said to be still slipping. Up to a year ago people were still allowed to climb to the top, but it is closed to the public now which must indicate that they are worried about its safety. For my own part, I was relieved about that since I had been up as many high, man-made structures as I ever intend. I hope to land in heaven one day, if there is such a place, but not quite yet! But I thought the Leaning Tower a lovely building, and I hope it does stay up.

The next leg of the journey took me through the most beautiful part of Tuscany, where they make the famous wine of the region – chianti. It is a place which has inspired many poets and painters with huge wooded valleys, hillsides covered in vines and all the horizons studded with dozens of varieties of the cypress tree, which is the symbol of Tuscany. Some of the views reminded me of Stainmore, which is one of the more attractive parts of Teesdale and the place where both my mother and father were raised as children. There are many more trees in Tuscany than Stainmore, of course, but there was definitely a certain resemblance.

The road wound its way through some really beautiful hill villages, quite ancient-looking and every one with a panoramic view of the valleys. And we fetched up in one called Volpaia, which someone said had existed since AD 1100. It was as pretty a village as I've ever seen and only thirty-two people lived there –

Hopefully, it will stay up.

and every one of the adults worked on making the Volpaia chianti, which I understand is renowned. It must be – they were charging passing tourists around £12 a bottle for some vintages.

I was taken on a tour of the estate by a very friendly couple called Tulleo – that was the husband – and his wife, Nuccia. I gathered that they managed the place, and that she was the wine taster, which meant that she must have had a deep know-ledge of the craft of making wine. We immediately found com-mon ground because they turned out to be as silly about dogs as me, and had several bouncing around the place. I made good friends with two of them, an extremely large but gentle kind of Old English sheep-dog called Dragon who was black, and a little thing like a miniature foxhound called Piccolo. They were in-terested to learn that I had been a farmer and wanted to know what I grew, so I told them that no one ever managed to grow a grape in Baldersdale! Anyway, I described how I raised beef cattle, and asked if they had any beasties hidden away some-where. It seems they used to have, judging from what our trans-lator said, around 3,000 rather unusual cattle in the Chianti region, with upturned pointed horns. They were used for haul-ing things, such as ploughs, so they must have been some kind of oxen. Anyway they had all gone now, replaced by mechan-ization in the sixties, and only around five survived.

Tulleo then wanted to show me his vines, and Nuccia had to hang on to me because the ground sloped away sharply and was quite rough and overgrown with grass. They explained that the shocking weather had prevented them from keeping the place tidy – it had, in fact, been the worst recorded weather for the time of the year for the last 120 years in Chianti. So that meant a poor harvest, for certain. But they both seemed quite cheerful about it and we went on to inspect the cellars, deep and dark with enormous double doors and locks to match. I'd never seen such a size of barrel in all my life – some must have been more than fifteen feet high. Tulleo drew a glass of gleaming red wine from one, and you could tell from his face how proud he was of it. Apparently Castello Volpaia wine is among the best from Chianti, and Tulleo was very understanding when I declined a taste. I had determined after the incident on the boat on the Seine in Paris that one taste of alcoholic liquid would be suffi-

Others tasted wine, I
stuck to Adam's ale!

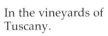

In the vineyards of
Tuscany.

The square in Siena where the Palio is run.

cient. When there was no tea or coffee available, people were usually able to find some good bottled water wherever I went – not the gassy stuff which doesn't suit me, just plain water.

My visit ended with a spread of tasty slices of salami carved by Nuccia, accompanied by some special biscuits made to a secret recipe, with all of us seated round an enormous table in what I presumed was the castello. Everyone else was enjoying the wine but I was happy with my Adam's ale, as we called it back home.

My next stop was in the nearby city of Siena, a very medieval place with narrow streets and very tall buildings. The buildings seemed very crowded together to me and the centre part revolved around a vast square called Piazza del Campo, which slopes about in a very uneven way. It is famous for a particular horse race they hold twice a year round the perimeter, called the Palio. Each district in the city enters an animal and apparently there is fierce competition, which leads to a lot of nasty accidents, since there isn't much room for a lot of galloping horses, and the clay track they lay down is hemmed in by stone buildings. I had my lunch in an open-air café right on the race track and got into conversation with a dark-haired, young English-speaking waiter, who told me about the excitement of last year's event. He was very anxious to point out the place where one horse had been killed when it had lost its rider and slammed straight into the wall at full pelt. Well, I didn't like this and I told him so. It's all right for the riders because they know the risks and have a choice, but the horses don't. They cannot say, No, I'm not going. They are just loyal and do their best. If I had a horse, and it was capable of winning the Grand National I wouldn't let it race. It seems that people pay as much as a hundred pounds each to watch the Palio, and I told the young man, who was called Ibrahim, that I wouldn't attend even if I was paid to do so. This, I am afraid, led to rather a difference of

Making up after the argument in Siena – the waiter extends a hand.

Sightseeing in Siena.

opinion with Ibrahim arguing that what did one horse matter when people were fighting and killing each other as they did in the Gulf, and thousands were starving in Africa. But I wouldn't accept this line of argument, and I think he got a bit upset because he turned on his heel and left me. I am glad to say, however, that we parted friends and when I got up to go he came over and gave me a kiss.

And that welcome gesture – I never like leaving somewhere under a cloud, so to speak – signalled the start of a very entertaining spectacle. As I left the café I heard the sound of singing and a large group of young people surged into the square. Most of them were dressed in velvet robes and hats with plumes, looking for all the world as if they were extras in a Shakespearian play. *Romeo and Juliet*, perhaps. They went to a café across the square where musicians started playing, so I joined the crowd gathering around them. There must have been a hundred altogether, eating, drinking and then dancing. It was a very jolly occasion, and I learned they were students celebrating the end of their first year in college.

So once again a visit ended musically, and I left Siena on the road for Rome, the Eternal City, taking the same path as Miss Furby again.

> *Ah Rome . . . The Forum . . . where still the eloquent air breathes . . . burns with Cicero.*

EXTRACT FROM THE JOURNAL OF MISS M.J. FURBY

Obviously Rome inspired my fellow Yorkshirewoman, because she had been more circumspect about Florence and other areas in her writings. I went immediately to the Forum. Now I know it's unique in its way, but I found it a strange and unusual place. I didn't exactly feel the warmth of Cicero, but the sun did come out for a while which was a welcome change. No, I'll not pretend that I even knew who Cicero was, because I'm not so good at history, and the significance of the Forum was a bit wasted on me. I didn't know what to think really. Apparently, they ran the Roman Empire from there and great names like Julius Caesar must have walked where I stood, but great Empires and great names crumble, don't they.

Afterwards I crossed the street to the Colosseum which I knew something about. Although it is a remarkable structure and must have been magnificent in its heyday when I believe it could seat seventy thousand people, I found it a grim place with such horrid associations. If only they had used if for nicer things, such as pantomimes. I just couldn't stop thinking about all those poor Christians being put to death. Probably many noble people saw the last light of day there.

The Colosseum affected Hannah's emotions to the extent that it appeared that she was about to shed tears at the memory of those early Christian martyrs. But the atmosphere was relieved by the intervention of two white-haired ladies from York, who delightedly

Meeting an admirer
also on a Roman
holiday.

A place with bad
associations – the
Colosseum.

Where history was
made – the Forum in
Rome, left.

homed in on Hannah and began clicking cameras and exchanging
travel tales, mostly unhappy. They had endured two weeks of rain
in Venice before proceeding to Rome. Other admirers of Hannah
had been encountered in the Forum and her celebrity status was
confirmed wherever she travelled. It was also noticeable how
warmly people who had no idea who Hannah was responded to
her. She seemed to bring out an affectionate, protective reaction
from waiters, porters, taxi-drivers, shopkeepers . . . just about
everyone she engaged in conversation, however brief. To a man –
or woman – they would beam with pleasure and go out of their way
to assist.

She has the power to create a very special atmosphere wherever she goes, whatever she does, and it is impossible to analyze.

The skies went black again as I left the Colosseum, and I saw
much of the rest of Rome from under an umbrella. I had a good
look at what the Romans call either the Wedding Cake or the
Typewriter, a somewhat extravagant memorial to both King
Victor Emmanuel II and the Italian Unknown Soldier from the
First World War, but then had to abandon sightseeing for the
day and seek shelter in the hotel. And to think that I had put on
my lilac summer dress with floppy hat decorated with a ribbon
to match, to celebrate the appearance of the sun in the morning,
which proved to be a very false dawn.

Perhaps even worse than the weather, and certainly more
alarming was the average Italian driver. Crossing the streets was
a real hazard. Cars, and particularly scooters, came at you from
all directions and seemed to obey no laws at all. It was even
worse than Paris, which was saying something.

However the night's events made up to a large extent for the
disappointment of the day when I was taken on a long taxi-ride
across the river which winds through Rome and into a rather
poor and dilapidated area called Trastevere. It is where they
have a lot of their celebrated theatre restaurants, and all tourists
are encouraged to go, and by my reckoning few will regret it. I
was fortunate enough to have an escort, from the Tourist Board,
a very presentable young man called Francesco Casertano, and
we dined in what must have once been a theatre, except that
they had taken out all the seats and replaced them with tables

The 'typewriter' which commemorates Italian war dead in Rome.

and chairs. But the stage was intact. It was called the Teatro Tiberino, and it filled up quickly with Japanese tourists, who were very polite and orderly. Francesco said it was more like downtown Tokyo than Rome! He told me he was born in Austria and had lived in many countries because he was the son of a diplomat – and what a talented linguist he turned out to be. He was fluent in Spanish, French, Italian and English, and had a family home in Tuscany as well as a place in Rome. We got on very well, and we talked amongst other things about dogs we had owned.

Sadly, he had recently lost a little spaniel to which he had been most attached. Still, the evening was a great success for me. I had a steak which was properly cooked for once, not red raw in the middle, and then we were entertained by a group of about fifteen musicians and singers who often came off the stage to wander around the tables. They were very loud but also very good, and they came to our table two or three times – indeed, not a table in the place was missed, so they had to work very hard. One gentleman with peculiar eyes sang and played the mandolin for me, but I much preferred a rather handsome tenor who serenaded me with 'Love's Last Word is Spoken, Cherie'. It was very much my style of entertainment, full of melody and lovely Italian songs like 'Santa Lucia', 'Arrivederci Roma' and 'Come Back to Sorrento'.

Next day I attempted to go sightseeing again and walked to the Spanish Steps from my hotel. It reminded me very much of Sacré-Coeur in the Montmartre area of Paris because the steps there were also full of young people sitting down, talking and eating pizzas. I think some were hoping to get a sun-tan but down came the rain once again. Still, I pressed on under a very jolly yellow and white umbrella, which, would you believe, I had acquired to protect me from the sun, because I was determined to see the Trevi fountain. By the time I reached it, a full-blooded thunderstorm was in progress and the curious thing was that, although there was water, water everywhere, the Trevi fountain had not a drop! They were in the middle of restoring the superb statues of Neptune and his attendants, sculpted by Bernini, I'm told, and the base was completely covered over with canvas. So . . . I was unable to throw a coin into the fountain to ensure, as the legend says, that I return to Rome. But considering the weather I experienced there I cannot say that I was much bothered.

7

Face to Face With Pope John Paul

In London, the principal aim of most tourists is to catch a glimpse of the Queen or some other member of the Royal Family. Which leads to a permanent disruption of traffic down the Mall to Buckingham Palace as thousands turn up each day to hang hopefully around the railings, watching the Changing of the Guard, and rushing forward eagerly to try and see who is in the cars allowed to enter and leave the wrought iron gates, just in case a royal might be on the move.

In Rome, of course, the majority of visitors want to see the Pope, who is more accessible than the Queen because he appears every Wednesday in St Peter's Square. Since Hannah had been to Buckingham Palace to a Garden Party and had made her curtsey to the Queen, an honour which she much appreciated, an attempt was made to bring Hannah into a position where she could both see and be photographed with His Holiness Pope John Paul. But, unless special arrangements are made, all a tourist can do is join the crowd at the entrance to the Square where the Pope is at best a white dot in the distance, and the intervening ground is covered with thousands of pilgrims.

A letter was written to the Vatican well in advance of Hannah's tour, explaining who Hannah Hauxwell was and respectfully requesting one of the reserved seats as near to the front as possible, but no reply was forthcoming. However, mid-way through Hannah's stay in Rome, a telephone call to the hotel led to negotiations with a certain American lady with much influence in these matters, who works in the Vatican's Council for Social Communications, Mrs Marjorie Weeks. She listened sympathetically to the proposition that Hannah's admirers would much appreciate an opportunity for her to see His Holiness, but could promise nothing. Just that she would do her best. Hannah was due to leave Rome on the day of the Pope's appearance, but the night before another telephone message asked Hannah to present herself at the Vatican at ten o'clock the next morning. Travel plans were hastily rearranged.

St Peter's Square was already filling up as a car whisked Hannah through a rear gate of the Vatican, and she was led through the ranks of nuns and robed priests in that small independent state, to a reserved seat at the edge of one section already filled to near capacity by an excited choir from Poland, the Pope's home country, and close by a squad of the Swiss Guards clad in those curious, candy-striped uniforms. The Yorkshire Television film

Pope John Paul arrives in St Peter's Square.

crew was placed on the top of a platform reserved for press and television reporters, and the only clear indication of exactly where Hannah was seated from that point was afforded by her white and yellow umbrella, being used at last for its proper purpose since the day was blessed throughout with hot sunshine. But special pleading led to Mostafa Hammuri, the cameraman, being allowed to stand close to Hannah with a hand-held camera. He was closely escorted throughout.

The excitement in St Peter's Square grew perceptibly as eleven o'clock, the appointed time for the Pope's appearance, drew nearer. An enormous group from Germany dressed in dark blue uniforms with pill box hats decked with red plumes played mightily on a selection of instruments, guitars could be heard from another quarter, and the air was filled with chanting, singing and music. The place erupted when Pope John Paul arrived from the Vatican, standing in his special jeep, which moved up and down the corridors carefully laid out to allow its proper progress, the Pope blessing the faithful and leaning over to touch hands. It was a

beautifully organized and moving spectacle. Hannah was properly impressed.

The German band in their fancy hats.

It was, indeed, a very special occasion and I was a most privileged person. I was close by the place where the Pope appeared in his little car, and got a fairly good view as he passed by, even though there were a lot of excited people pushing and crowding around to get a better look. It was understandable though, because they were Polish, the Pope's own people. I was quite frightened for a while but a very kind couple from New Jersey in the United States became my companions and also thoughtfully appointed themselves my guardians, and protected me when the others were surging around. My, but there was a noise as the Pope drove slowly up and down, until he went to his rostrum and began his address, which he read out from a prepared text in all manner of languages. He said, in the English version, that he had just returned from a pilgrimage to

Portugal where he had gone to give thanks at a special shrine for being saved from death ten years ago, which I assumed was when an assassin had attempted to take his life.

Then his assistant read out the names of some of the groups among the audience, and named the countries from where they came, and many of them rose to sing or cheer and play music. The German band in the fancy hats played more than once and there were many pauses in the ceremony as the Pope listened to various choirs singing to him. Other groups just jumped up and down and waved when they were mentioned and the Pope acknowledged them all with a big smile and a wave. I found it quite moving when the Polish choir alongside me rose and sang so beautifully, and I could tell that he was especially pleased to welcome his fellow country folk.

The Pope speaking from the podium.

Pope John Paul greets
the pilgrims.

Mostafa Hammuri
filming the Pope, left.

It all went on for some hours and the heat was quite intense. And the atmosphere became even more electric when that part of the ceremony finished and the Pope rose from his great chair and moved down to greet lots of people personally. He was surrounded by the Vatican's own cameramen and security guards. I suppose his bodyguards must be very anxious when he does that because he is so vulnerable, and it's already been proved what a single madman can do. One lady became a bit overexcited and rose from her seat to run towards him, but she was intercepted and pushed gently back. The Pope must have noticed because he came up to her and gave her a special blessing, putting his hand on her head. The gesture obviously thrilled her.

The Pope noticeably spent more time with the children, being held up to him, and with people in wheelchairs. It must be very tiring giving an audience like that every Wednesday, and he was so diligent and caring. I don't think he missed anybody out, and he never stopped smiling. I am not a Roman Catholic, but I have always liked the look of Pope John Paul and he fulfilled all my expectations.

But I certainly didn't expect what happened next. He came closer and closer, and then began greeting the Polish contingent, so I was able to get a really good look at him in close-up. He appeared older and smaller than I had imagined, quite frail to undergo all that pressure and tumult. The Poles were quite beside themselves with joy to meet him and the pushing and shoving started around me again and I lost sight of him.

And then . . . there he was, right in front of me. Pope John Paul himself, face to face with Hannah Hauxwell! He held out his hands to me and I took his left hand in mine.

Now that's a moment which will live with me. A true privilege.

8

Trials and Tribulations Behind the Scenes

In order to give a more rounded account of my adventures I need to describe some of the events which occurred behind the scenes during the filming by Yorkshire Television of my tour of Europe. Of course, I soon found out that travelling abroad has its painful moments, however well organized, with queues, waiting about and frequent dashes to make the next connection.

But with twenty-three boxes of filming equipment weighing half a ton, plus all the personal luggage, it is quite another matter. It is not easy for a film crew to progress from one country to another under any circumstances, and the way I chose to go created unusual and unforeseen problems. Almost always, a crew will arrive by air; occasionally by road. But I had opted for train travel and railway lines do not always cross frontiers at a

The aptly named porter, Mr Pilgrim, at Victoria Station.

The adventure is about
to begin.

Dover next stop.

convenient place for the Customs people. Now, for most of us all
you need is a passport and an honest face, but film crews have to
carry something called a carnet. It is a bundle of documents
about three inches thick which lists every item carried in the

boxes, down to the last power battery for the sound recorder. One hundred and fifty-nine items in total! When you cross a border the carnet must be stamped out by the officials of the country you are leaving, and stamped in by the officials of the country you are entering. Miss just one part of that double act and you can land in real trouble.

Everything was made worse by the unpleasant discovery that the railway porter appears to be an endangered species. In certain parts of Europe they have even become extinct. In Zürich, for instance, only one survives. He has no mate at all. In Basle, the porter is but a fond memory. None has been spotted for years!

Now the rail travel began well enough at Victoria Station, London, where the good Mr Pilgrim was just one of a happy and willing group of porters. There were teams of strong young men in Calais and Paris, too. But everything went wrong when we arrived in Cologne on the train from Paris one Saturday night. From then on it became a nightmare.

The train had crossed the border from France into Germany with no sign of a Customs man, but the crew were assured that

A short nap on the way to Paris.

Arriving in Paris . . .
and later, filming in
the Place du Tertre.

such controls didn't exist any more with the dawn of a United Europe, but there was a feeling of much unease. This turned to panic when we embarked from the train in Cologne and discovered that the luggage van had simply disappeared! And it was carrying all our personal luggage as well as the camera equipment. The poor crew went up and down the train like mad things trying to find out what had happened, but the single railway official on the platform just wasn't interested.

Neither were there any porters. Not one. But two men with trolleys from the Dom Hotel were waiting to meet us. However, we had nothing to hand over to them. Not even a toothbrush! The management of the Dom were most efficient and helpful, ringing around everywhere they could, passing on to the railway authorities a message from our producer/director, Barry Cockcroft, that legal action would be taken if our property was not returned forthwith. There was deep depression when the news came through that the luggage van had been traced – but was on its way to Copenhagen, and that the train's final destination was Moscow. However, they were trying to stop the train in Düsseldorf to remove our belongings. Then there was a message to say that it had been stopped, but no one was prepared to transport anything back to Cologne for us. It was past midnight by then, but a taxi was called and half the crew charged off to Düsseldorf, leaving the other half trying to sort out the Customs clearances. A phone call from the rescue party revealed that our personal luggage was there, but of the camera gear not a sign. Nor any clue as to where it was. Then the hotel night manager received a call to say that it was on its way from Münster to Cologne and would arrive at 3.40 a.m. – but the train would stop for three minutes only! Two of the Dom Hotel porters were roused from their beds and all able-bodied members of our team were on the platform, waiting anxiously at the spot where they had been told the luggage van would stop. It was bitterly cold, the train was late – and the van stopped as far away from the nominated place as it was possible. I was told that those three minutes were among the most frantic of the tour, as twenty-three boxes were unceremoniously hauled off. Only small luggage trolleys were available and it took several difficult journeys to get everything to the hotel, so it was nearly five o'clock in the morning before the crisis was over and those poor, exhausted people got to bed. I must point out here that I was protected from most of the ordeal and only heard the details the next day.

The Dom management eventually offered a very unusual explanation for the episode. Apparently they had been told that German Customs were expecting drug smugglers to try clever new ways of getting their evil merchandise across the border, and concluded that we might be a group pretending to be a film crew with all the right equipment, except that the cases of film and lenses would be concealing cocaine or heroin. They wanted to part us from the gear for a while so that sniffer dogs could check everything – the cases were not locked. But no dogs had been available in Cologne when the train arrived, so the twenty-three cases had been removed and taken swiftly to the military base at Münster where they did have dogs. The general opinion was that this was a very clever story concocted to try and avoid a claim for damages.

The next border we crossed – at a very early hour in the morning – was between Germany and Switzerland on the Rhine cruise. The crew kept their heads low so as far as the carnet was concerned we never visited Germany at all. It said we were still in France. The Swiss Customs man was a very pleasant gentleman and stamped us into his country with a smile, but the vehicles which were supposed to meet us to take everything to the railway station at Basle never turned up. So the next crisis developed. We originally had a comfortable three hours to get from the boat to the station, a distance of less than a mile, but we had less than twenty minutes to spare when we finally arrived there. Porters were called for, but we were told that none existed at all. Eventually the guard of our train was alerted and he and a companion managed to find a large trolley and, with two minutes to go before the train's departure, that trolley came down the platform at a dangerous speed. In desperation Barry Cockcroft even ran to the engine driver to try and negotiate a little more time, and the last box was heaved on board with thirty seconds to spare. The guard telegraphed ahead to Geneva to warn them of our arrival, and assurances were given that a willing team of men would be waiting to assist, and that there would be plenty of time to unload before the train resumed its journey. But when

we got there, the platform was deserted. And then we were informed that there would, once more, be a stop of just three minutes. So the desperate scramble began all over again with Barry Cockcroft standing by with one hand on the emergency stop lever, fully prepared to risk the consequences.

A quick crew conference was called as soon as everyone had recovered enough energy to speak, and it was unanimously decided to avoid rail travel like the plague from then on. In one way it was a pity, because Thomas Cook had been careful to book seats on some very special trains, all with romantic names like the 'Maria Theresia' to Salzburg, the 'Schonbrunn' to Vienna, and the 'Romulus' to Rome. But everyone was prepared to drive very long distances to avoid the risk of the entire enterprise collapsing. That, plus the fact that it is, apparently, far easier to cross national borders by road, since you are not governed by the timetable of the train.

The wisdom of that was severely tested when we arrived at the French border to go back into Switzerland, just outside

Conversation with Barry Cockcroft.

Geneva. The Swiss Customs people became very agitated because their colleague in Basle, pleasant though he was, had apparently not carried out his part properly. Not signed in duplicate, or something like that. So the Swiss officials totally refused to have anything to do with us, so we passed through to the French side to see what they had to say. That led to a lot of gesticulation and exasperated comments in rapid French, and for some agonizing minutes we thought we would have to backtrack all the way to Basle to sort the matter out. Which would have been disastrous because much of the detailed research and carefully timed preparations would have been ruined if just one day had been lost.

But that is when we played our ace card. She is called Ann Maguire, a slim little thing with big green eyes, who did a won-

Ann Maguire, our assistant cameraperson.

derful job as assistant to our cameraman, Mostafa Hammuri (the Great Mostafa, of course). The French are clearly more susceptible to feminine charm than the Swiss, who were much more formal and stiff, and after shouting a little and threatening to impose a substantial fine, finally scored out the entry made by the Swiss man at Basle and allowed us to proceed. Ann rewarded them with a tearful smile.

From then on it was more a case of tedious waiting about at borders rather than facing more crises. Our little transit van had to queue up with the truck drivers and juggernauts at national boundaries. They never seemed to have enough people to deal swiftly with the paperwork, so all those poor drivers must spend a substantial proportion of their working lives standing in line. We had language problems as well as being an unusual cargo,

Barry Cockcroft and Kathy Rooney on the Orient Express.

Mostafa Hammuri
behind the camera.

Chris Greaves, our
sound recordist.

and little Ann got us through. The rest of the crew soon learned to stay out of the way as Ann, so waiflike and vulnerable with those green eyes as big as saucers, joined in with all those big swarthy men, all denims and moustaches, and had them running around helping out with translations, and old-world courtesy. You could always tell by the smile on the face of the Customs men that things were going well. It was very wearisome sitting there for hour after hour, and not even a cup of tea to sustain you. But the good humour of my very dear friend, the indispensable Kathy Rooney, who has been co-ordinating Barry Cockcroft's programmes for nearly twenty years, and our young sound recordist Chris Greaves, lifted our spirits. Chris, by the way, is a qualified pilot and flying instructor as well as being a skilled driver of more mundane vehicles.

One day, because the motorway we had to use crossed from Switzerland into Germany, then from Germany into Austria, the normal journey time was quadrupled which meant that we arrived in Salzburg late at night, and completely worn out.

Getting into Italy was reasonably trouble free because the Italian Customs men responded with even more enthusiasm than the French to Ann's charm. From then on we thankfully had no more national frontiers to cross until we joined the Orient Express in Venice (after driving the best part of three thousand miles in two vehicles provided by Hertz). The management of that superb train took everything over, passports as well as the carnet, and saw us smoothly through Italy into France while we relaxed and enjoyed ourselves.

9

See Naples and Cry …

There is probably not in the wide world a city more beautifully situated than that of Naples . . . and there is a proverb in use to express the charms of the locality . . . 'See Naples and Die'.

EXTRACT FROM THE JOURNAL OF MISS M.J. FURBY

I went up the hill to San Martino and had a good look at the same view which Miss Furby had found so thrilling. But I was soaking wet through when I came to it because the rain clouds which had followed me all through Europe turned up once again and caught me out in the open. Naples was to be the southernmost point in my travels, and Barry Cockcroft had

See Naples ... and cry!

A hat in peril
overlooking Naples.

declared during the downpour in Rome that if the sun didn't
shine in Naples I may see a grown man cry! So I said as I looked
down at a distinctly damp city, that it was a case of 'See Naples
and Cry . . . '!

There wasn't a lot to see of the islands as Capri and Ischia were
under cloud – and so was Vesuvius – but the sight of all those
buildings hemmed in by the mountains was certainly spectacular, although it could have done with a few more trees and a bit
of greenery here and there.

As I looked at it I was reminded of a saying which my uncle

used to come out with now and again: 'See Naples and Die? . . . No, I'd rather see Paris and Live!' At the time I fully agreed with him.

End of a damp drive in Naples, with Fulvia.

The day had started well enough at the Hotel Britannique, a very old and spacious establishment, with its own glorious view of the Bay of Naples. It was just the sort of place Miss Furby would have stayed at, and maybe did, and displayed on the wall by the reception area was an old notice for British travellers listing the various attractions and excursions available for tourists. The owner of the hotel, a Dr Giovanni Ambrosi, who welcomed me personally with old-fashioned courtesy, told me he had found it among his grandfather's papers, and it would be around a hundred years old. His family had owned the hotel all that time. The notice advertised train journeys to Pompeii lasting one hour, or a two-hour carriage ride – 'fatiguing' it said – and the admission was five lire. The National Museum was only two lire to enter, so I imagine they were not offering two thousand lire to the pound in those days.

The poster also mentioned a 'glorious afternoon carriage drive' through the city to the hill of San Martino, and I was pleased to find out that this facility was still available, so a horse and carriage were summoned. I was just about to climb aboard it with my very knowledgeable guide, Mrs Fulvia Filangieri, when it suddenly began to pour down. So a poor horse once again had to stand and wait in the wet until it stopped. There was enough water running down the gutters for it to have a long drink.

The ride started eventually under leaden skies and we trotted through the crazy traffic back to the promenade by the sea. I didn't care much for that beast which was decidedly temperamental and reared up once or twice, although you could scarcely blame it in all that confusion on the roads. Fulvia was trying her best to explain about some of the sights we were trying to take in, but with all the hooting of horns and the screeching scooters tearing around taking all manner of risks quite a lot of what she said was lost. But I did manage to hear an interesting story about a castle which had once stood by the sea in Naples, known locally as the Egg Castle. It was called that because of a prediction by the poet Virgil who lived in Naples and was apparently regarded by the Neapolitans as something of a magician – rather like our own Merlin, I imagine. Fulvia said he placed a box of eggs somewhere in the castle and declared that if they were broken the entire place would fall down. Eventually there was an earthquake, the eggs fell and the remains of the castle now lie under the sea. Not such a brilliant prediction when you consider how prone the area is to that kind of disaster. Fulvia told me about the last serious earthquake, which was as recent as 1980, and what a terrifying experience it had been for her. Her house trembled like a leaf, all the pottery jumped up around the place and the pictures on the wall finished up hanging all askew. She and her family stayed in the garden all day, only daring to go in the house to switch on the television to see the news about the damage and whether any more tremors were predicted – watching through the window. They slept in their car for three nights, and it turned out they didn't need the television to warn them about impending tremors. Just before they happened the dogs around the area would start quivering and whining and the water in their well – they had a private one, forty metres deep – would begin roaring and surging up.

That story made me a mite nervous about being in the region, a feeling which was definitely increased when another downpour forced us to abandon the journey by horse and carriage and we took to a taxi to see the rest of the city.

> *That which deeply interests the traveller at Naples, is not buildings, but life. The place is packed with vivacious life. How they managed to find subsistence is difficult to discover.*

EXTRACT FROM THE JOURNAL OF MISS M.J. FURBY

It most certainly is packed with life in the old part of the city, but it is scarcely vivacious. Fulvia took care to lock all the doors in the taxi, saying it was a dangerous place full of people looking for a chance to snatch your belongings. If you walked around that area with handbags or cameras it was odds on that someone would try to cut through the straps or rifle your pockets, disappearing immediately up one of the maze of dark and narrow alley-ways.

But it was still true, as Miss Furby pointed out, that it was difficult to imagine how they survived. Fulvia said that large families of about ten children were commonplace, so there was a lot of poverty and overcrowding. Still, there was one thing to be said in favour of the situation – they were good to the old folk, and didn't push them off to a Home somewhere. Their style of living may be hard, with sheer survival the major driving force, but the elders were treated with love and respect. It was a confusing experience with high, dilapidated tenements with washing hanging everywhere, standing alongside some wonderful old palaces, with courtyards and fountains. The place just seethes with colour and noise and squalor – and the inevitable scooters.

Fulvia took me to her home in the evening to meet her husband and three daughters, not to mention their puppy dog which was light in colour and like a labrador. She had a lovely spacious apartment not far from the Royal Palace. I had a teaspoon of some of her home-made wine, so as not to offend, although I did not consider it broke my resolve to avoid alcohol in future, not really.

Fulvia's youngest daughter, Constanza, had been searching

for us all day because she had been anxious to see us riding in the *carnozzella* (the horse and carriage) and had kept missing us as we slowly manoeuvred our way through the crowded streets and along the bay.

Fulvia and her husband also owned a house near the sea and a place in the country where they had vineyards. It was interesting to hear that the vineyards produced three crops – I understood that under the vines producing the grapes they also grew aubergines, and below them potatoes – which I thought was a very useful way to use the land. Obviously they were a wealthy family, and I subsequently learned that Fulvia was actually a contessa – her full name was Fulvia Filangieri di Candida.

Fortune at last began to favour us the next day when the sun made a belated appearance, although there was a keen little wind nevertheless, and we went to visit Pompeii. Now I must admit that I wasn't exactly excited at the prospect of viewing some more ruins which – such as the Forum – don't appear to have any shape or meaning because only bits of masonry and the odd column have survived. At least they don't say anything special to me, although that's my own fault – I should have studied a lot more of the history of the Roman Empire.

Pompeii was altogether different. I thought it out of this world. It's so complete you can imagine how it was the day Vesuvius erupted and snuffed it out like a candle. You can almost feel the presence of the people who inhabited it – indeed, some are still there, petrified into a kind of stone by the lava dust and poisonous gasses that hit them on that terrible afternoon on the 24 August AD 79. They can pin-point almost to the hour from the surviving records of the time.

It must have been sudden because they found bread still on the table by the side of the oven in one of the baker's shops.

It was truly a tragic town because it had been badly damaged by an earthquake only seventeen years beforehand. I saw some of the bodies, but I didn't get the uncomfortable feeling that I was looking at a dead person because they appeared to have been carved by a sculptor. Except for one, that is, who had a good set of real teeth showing in a kind of agonized grimace. Poor man. He was believed to be a slave in the Bath House where the excavators found him, because he was wearing the

Among the inspirational ruins of Pompeii, exploring the Forum and the Main Street, with Vesuvius in the background.

sort of belt around his middle which slaves were made to wear. So he couldn't have had much of a life.

I was told there were thermal baths, by the way, with a warm pool, a cold plunge and even a kind of sauna. All that luxury two thousand years ago, which is amazing when you consider that my farm in Baldersdale didn't even have cold running water until a couple of years ago, when the people who bought it sank a well successfully.

Fulvia told me that Pompeii had obviously been a prosperous town with a good trade in wool and could boast two theatres, a forum, a basilica, and even a stock exchange. A lot of the columns had been clad in marble, a very skilled kind of workmanship and another sign of wealth, and it was also famous for having carved stepping-stones across the sunken paved streets which meant the citizens could keep their feet dry when they crossed to the raised pavements during heavy rain. If you painted them white they would look just like pedestrian crossings. Fulvia was also keen to show me an archway decorated in the most delicate of carved marble, featuring tiny, beautifully fashioned birds, rabbits and even a snail. It was protected by thick glass from the elements – and vandals. I was told that they had been obliged to remove many of the more vulnerable objects, such as bits of bread in the bakery and small household objects, to the Museum in Naples because so many things have been stolen.

By the way Pompeii does have some inhabitants – a pack of dogs with, unfortunately, no owners. They are all shapes and sizes and sometimes barked a lot. I was told the restaurant gives them food but otherwise they just do the best they can, poor things.

The most fascinating of all the buildings I saw was the house of two rich brothers called Vettii, who were wine merchants, which was one of the more recent discoveries. It had a sunken area in the entrance which may have been a fountain, with decorated bedrooms leading off and the prettiest of gardens in the middle of cloisters. It seemed they had gone to the trouble of identifying the seeds found in the original garden and had repeated it exactly – they must have had roses in those days because I saw several bushes in bloom. They also found a marble

Lunchtime in Pompeii with Fulvia.

Thomas Cook, with a
group he took to
Pompeii more than a
century ago.
*Courtesy of Thomas Cook
Archives*

table and little bronze statues and placed them where they had
been when the house was completely covered to a depth of at
least five metres. The house was also thought remarkable for the
variety and interest of the wall paintings, featuring mythological
scenes in the main, and they were remarkably fresh and colourful when you consider just what they had been through.

I don't think the Vettii house had been properly excavated in
Mr Thomas Cook's time. He personally led several parties of his
clients to Pompeii and I have seen a very interesting group photo
taken all those years ago alongside one of the houses, with the
great excursionist himself in the centre. Incidentally, I made an
acquaintance in the Forum with modern-day tourists. Two
ladies spotted me and came over for a chat. One was from Black-
pool and the other from Newcastle. The latter lady said she
recognized my voice before she even saw me, so I must have
been chattering away at the time.

Pompeii is, of course, dominated by the bulk of Vesuvius, the
volcano which both took its life and preserved its body for the
enjoyment and education of subsequent generations – and I
must say that my visit to Pompeii was definitely one of the highlights of my entire tour, really wonderful. I would love to spend
more time there. Even the lunch I ate at the restaurant, cleverly

built inside one of the original structures so as not to strike a false note, was one of the best I ate in my stay in the Bay of Naples. On all counts, therefore, I can recommend Pompeii since it is unique in the whole world and I would urge anyone to seize any chance to view it.

The next obvious stop on any visit to the area was Vesuvius. It was a long drive up another of one of those steep and winding roads I disliked so much in Switzerland. And on the way up most of the bushes and greenery dwindled away and the landscape was made very sinister by the petrified rivers of lava from the various eruptions, just like vast fields of cinders. The Valley of Hell they called it, which I thought a very apt description. It certainly made my blood run cold, particularly when I heard Vesuvius had last thrown a fit in 1944, and came close to wiping out another community.

... and it was active in those days, too!
Courtesy of Thomas Cook Archives

... as far as I intend to go up Vesuvius!

Cold to the entire body it was, too, when we arrived at the spot where vehicles can go no further, because it is about 3,000 feet high and the air is thin and the temperature low. I heard one man in the café where I warmed up with a cappuccino complaining about the cold, and he turned out to hail from Finland! And there was a bit of a peculiar smell hanging about the place.

There used to be a funicular railway to the very edge of the crater, which is 700 metres in circumference, but it was no longer working, and if you want to get to peer over the edge it is necessary to walk the last stage. A man was offering to rent out climbing sticks, and Fulvia asked me if I would like to go, but I swiftly declined her kind offer. Lots of people were trekking laboriously up along paths criss-crossing the lava, and I know it was a popular thing – almost obligatory – in Thomas Cook's day. There was even a song written about the climb to Vesuvius, entitled 'Cook's Excursion Galop', and the song-sheet had a very amusing cartoon depicting his clients tumbling about the place. I imagine that Thomas might have been a trifle old for such excursions at the time because the man featured in the centre of the cartoon was his son. They had some nerve, those early British tourists, because the volcano must have been active in those days. Apparently, it has not emitted any smoke since 1944, but it was still a menacing thing to me. It may appear to be dormant, but you can never tell.

I was glad to have had the opportunity to make the acquaintance of Vesuvius, but even more pleased to bid it farewell. It put me a bit on edge. And would you believe, there was a loud thunderstorm – yet again – the following afternoon and I hurried to my bedroom window to make sure that the ugly old monster wasn't stirring again.

10

On Stilts to Capri …
and the Ordeal of the
Blue Grotto

Hannah's trip to Capri was, in the planning stage, considered likely to be one of the pleasanter, less taxing parts of her stay in the Bay of Naples. What had been totally forgotten was the lady's complete lack of close acquaintance with the sea. Crossing the Channel in a large and luxurious boat, almost totally distanced from the water since it was half a skyscraper in height, had in no way prepared her for an unexpected development when she embarked, as Miss Furby had done a century or more ago, on a visit to the Blue Grotto. The morning was deceptively beautiful – warm sun and azure skies – but the improbably bad weather throughout Europe had left its legacy around the shores of Capri. The sea was clearly troubled, and when the Blue Grotto was approached after a choppy twenty-minute trip by launch, the YTV crew was horrified to see a struggling mass of small boats laden with wide-eyed and worried tourists making a decidedly perilous entry into the cave. The rise and fall of the sea closed the entrance to less than two feet at the top of the surge, and entry required expert timing by the boatmen, hauling the craft through by a chain, their passengers lying flat on the bottom of the boat. All eyes turned to Hannah, who was watching this spectacle with a face like stone, but saying not a word, and it was fully expected that the Blue Grotto would have to be cancelled. But she went through with it, although clearly hating every moment, which is a marvellous example of bravery from a lady made prematurely frail by the harsh life she led for so long, and who never in her life had been in a small boat before.

Oddly enough, the only minor concern at the start of the day had centred on Hannah's reaction to the hydrofoil, which sped her from Naples harbour to Capri.

Oh, I liked the hydrofoil. It was quite exciting, suddenly gathering speed and rising up on stilts. I felt very comfortable on it. I was also happy to meet a very engaging Italian couple from Rome who sat opposite me, and when they saw me being filmed, asked if I was famous. I told them that was not the case, and that I was just a simple Daleswoman from Yorkshire. They were involved with travel magazines, and had a holiday place on Capri and even asked me to stay with them if ever I returned to Rome – which, of course, may not happen,

A too close encounter
with the sea on the
way to the Blue Grotto.

And ... getting closer
to the ordeal!

since circumstances prevented me from throwing a coin into the Trevi fountain.

No, the problems started when we arrived at the harbour in Capri, and I was obliged to get into an open launch. I should have realized that a boat trip was necessary, but I confess I hadn't given it a thought. Now I had never been on the sea in such a craft before and the mighty ocean seemed a bit too near for my liking. Nor was I much comforted by the boatman saying that we must hurry to get aboard because the weather forecast was not very good. His boat seemed such a delicate craft, but I completely revised my opinion of it afterwards because I had to transfer to a little cocky thing to enter the Grotto, and a bonny pantomime there was getting me into that.

Going through that little hole in the wall was perhaps the worst moment of the entire trip, and that includes the Mer de Glace at Chamonix, and the dreaded Prater wheel in Vienna. Kathy Rooney came with me, and the boatman instructed us to lie down in the boat, or our heads would have collided with the rock. Once inside, after the nightmare of being dragged through on the chain when the sea fell back for a second or two, I still did not appreciate the situation. I admit the brilliant blue colour was clearly very thrilling to the people bobbing around in the other boats, and it is strange that it should reflect like it does, but I found it all eerie. I prefer the sky above me – enclosed places do nothing for my nervous system. I kept my head down all the time, just praying for the ordeal to be over.

Hannah was interviewed 'on the spot' many times during her tour but the one attempted in the Blue Grotto probably set some sort of television record for its brevity.

'Well, Hannah we made it. We're in the Grotto. What do you think?'

Silence

'Do you like it, Hannah?'

The reply snapped back in an unusual bass profundo.

'No . . . oo.'

End of interview.

Miss Furby, Hannah's worthy predecessor, reported rapturously about her visit to the same place.

Capri . . . of the many caves which the restless waves have hollowed out from the cliffs, the Grotta Azzurra – the Blue Grotto – is the most famous.

The effect of the reflected light entering the Grotto through the water from below is wonderful . . . Everything above water seems enveloped in a haze of the deepest azure . . . the coral reefs, water plants, and fish below seemed wrought of silver.

EXTRACT FROM THE JOURNAL OF MISS M.J. FURBY

I am sorry that I made a poor substitute for Miss Furby. She must have had a great taste for thrills. I was just very glad to get out of that place, although I have to admit that the journey back wasn't as bad as the scramble to get in, and I was lucky enough to avoid getting wet. Most other people were drenched from the sea bouncing off the sides on the way in, so my boatman must have been quite skilful. And my . . . what a joy it was to get back into the launch, which had worried me so on the way to the Grotto! It seemed so large and secure by comparison then.

But the rest of Capri made up in part for that experience. At first, when we arrived in the harbour, I thought that maybe the place wasn't quite what it was cracked up to be, famed in song and legend, like it is. However, I travelled in a lovely open car to Ana Capri at the top of the island and began to appreciate why people as diverse as the Roman Emperor Tiberius, and our own Gracie Fields had chosen to make their homes there. The views were quite wonderful and I liked the town and its quaint narrow streets, with flowers everywhere.

Capri increases in its dramatic beauty the higher you proceed, and the intention was to take Hannah to the very peak, Monte Solaro, which commands a stunning view of the entire Bay of Naples, from Vesuvius to Sorrento. What had been overlooked in the preliminary research – again – was that the only way to get there, unless you opted for an extremely arduous hill climb rising steeply to a height of 1,800 feet above sea level, was a chair lift. And what a chair lift it turned out to be. Certainly, not the gentle, spacious double chairs common on ski slopes, that remain stationary until you are com-

Exploring the narrow streets of Capri.

Overlooking Capri harbour, right.

fortably seated and then move on sedately. This one had single chairs of meagre dimensions and it was necessary to jump swiftly on to a small circle painted on the ground and look back anxiously as it sped towards your posterior. The pause when it arrived was minimal, and because the cable didn't stop at all, the chair lurched forward quite violently as it commenced the twelve-minute journey to the top. And from a distance, the final leg of the mountain appeared to be extremely steep. The look of horror on Hannah's face when she beheld this method of conveyance – which is perfectly safe and no problem for all those not of a nervous disposition – actually outstripped that displayed at the entrance to the Blue Grotto.

Tickets had been purchased, and all the film crew stood ready to go, festooned with the gear, but it was immediately apparent that Hannah must be allowed time and opportunity to decide whether to go or not. For at least five minutes she stood and watched a happy stream of tourists pile on board, gasping audibly as the first two or three launched into space. A small dog finally clinched the issue. It was being carried by its owner, who was in the queue, and Hannah was scandalized to such an extent that it was fortunate that the man didn't understand English.

'Oh, no! . . .' she exclaimed. 'The poor, wee thing. It doesn't have a choice.' And became even more agitated as it swung away up the mountain, protesting anxiously until it disappeared from sight.

'Well, you do have a choice, Hannah. And we don't think you really want to go, do you?'

Those were the words Hannah wanted to hear. Loyal to the end, she would have endured it had the television programme really required it. She was enormously relieved to miss the experience.

Well, you see, there wasn't much of substance around you on that little thing, and once you started there was no chance to change your mind and go back. Being perched at a height like that would have terrified me and I just hope that little dog got back safely. But missing out on the trip to the top of Monte Solaro gave us time we wouldn't otherwise have had to visit the Villa San Michele.

It's a wonderful old place, created by author Axel Munthe, who wrote the classic, *The Story of San Michele*. Although it was

A view from the Villa
San Michele and
rainclouds
approaching.

On the quayside, where the boats go to and from Naples and Capri.

first published in 1929, it is still popular, and has been translated into over fifty languages, I'm told. I confess to not having read it myself, but the house and garden he painstakingly restored are a dream. The villa is full of priceless furniture and sculptures, including a red granite sphinx from Egypt which is around 3,000 years old. And it is so peaceful and cool with fountains and courtyards and works of art everywhere, all very tastefully displayed.

The garden must be one of the finest in the whole of Italy, with an avenue of cypress trees, and a view from the pergola which just takes your breath away. The steep drop from the wall was a trifle worrying, but you can see all the way to Sorrento and watch the boats to-ing and fro-ing in the harbour below, tiny as a child's toys from that distance.

I spent a happy hour or so in the Villa San Michele, and for the first part the sun shone brilliantly, and then . . . the skies darkened and occasional flashes of lightning could be seen on the horizon. Again! It was hard to believe. But a local resident informed me that, although Capri had been inflicted with the worst start to the summer for many years, I should not complain. The previous day, snow had actually fallen in Calabria, which is much further south than Capri. It just goes to prove that there is always someone worse off than you.

It was raining steadily by the time I reached the harbour, and I boarded the hydrofoil back to Naples with the yellow and white umbrella performing yet again a task for which it was not originally required!

11

Venice …
Love at First Sight

No place is so beautiful as Naples . . . excepting Venice.
Everywhere you drink in its charm, subtle intoxication
and glory.

EXTRACT FROM THE JOURNAL OF MISS M.J. FURBY

For the very first time on my travels I found myself in complete agreement with my Victorian predecessor. Miss Furby, writing in 1877, was accurate in every way about Venice, which I found entrancing from the first moment I saw it. It was, without doubt, a case of love at first sight. It was dark when I arrived there and the magic began under a full moon. I caught my first glimpse of the Piazza San Marco, all bathed in floodlights, with the water of the lagoon shimmering like molten gold. Some measure of the effect it had on me can be gathered from the fact that, although the night was distinctly chilly and I am well known for my eagerness to keep warm, because I do feel the cold since I retired from the farm, I left the comfort and shelter of the cabin to go out and drink it all in. It was a chance too good to be missed.

And when the night was fairly come, you lay your head
upon the pillow with a smile – your last thought, 'I am in
Venice and tomorrow I shall see her beloved beauty again'.

EXTRACT FROM THE JOURNAL OF MISS M.J. FURBY

The next morning confirmed my opinion of Venice. It is absolutely wonderful, a dream . . . has to be seen to be believed. Just like stepping into the sixteenth century. I am not really one to be transported back in time in my imagination, but this place would inspire anybody. At any moment you expected to see Shylock hurrying by to get the latest news from the Rialto. And to think that many of the foundations of those beautiful palaces and churches are built on tree trunks, sunk centuries ago into the mud. Keeping the place afloat, I suppose, because I know that Venice is said to be sinking and in real danger. I do hope not, because this is certainly one place to which I truly wish to return.

Perhaps modern technology will come to the rescue and make it safe for future generations, and provide them with the pleasure which seeing Venice has given to me.

It is such a joy to walk about the streets – paved walkways really, since the streets are underwater! – without having to worry about traffic. So different from places like Rome and Naples where I was frightened to cross from one side of the road to the other. A thought did occur to me, however, that people would have to take care not to drink too much alcoholic refreshment or they might miss the bridges and walk into a canal! Mind, just looking at the buildings could have the same effect because they are quite intoxicating in their beauty. Such intricately carved stonework, frescos and tall columns. Some of the buildings even had paintings on the outside walls, let alone the inside.

My tour of Venice started in its most spectacular and historic place, the Piazza San Marco, or St Mark's Square. I approached it on my first morning by the very best way – by launch across the lagoon, landing at the entrance, which they call the Piazzetta, or ante-chamber. It is there that the symbols of Venice tower above you, the twin columns bearing the winged lion of San Marco on one, and the statue of Saint Theodore, the first Patron Saint of the city before Saint Mark, on the other. And to think that they were first set up on the same spot in 1172. But there is a dark side to this lovely place, because it was the scene of public executions. I was told that they still keep two oil-lamps burning nearby in memory of a poor baker's boy who was put to death after being accused unjustly of murdering a nobleman. Not much compensation though, is it?

From there you walk past St Mark's Library and the Doge's Palace – a particularly striking building, so white and delicate, like icing sugar – and turn left into the main square. The thing to do there is buy a packet of corn to feed the pigeons and have your photograph taken. I've done that in Trafalgar Square, but the experience here is multiplied several times. Those birds get everywhere, and they were almost fearless. I was quite taken aback by their numbers and persistence. You can really get dizzy here coping with the pigeons and taking in the amazing sights all around you. There was a clock tower with two enormous

A photo session with the pigeons in St Mark's Square.

155

green men with hammers with which they bang a large bell. In fact, there is such a melodic din when they start, and five bells in the tower, 320 feet above the square, join in too.

The history of the Square is really remarkable. It's seen such incident, both triumph and tragedy, down the ages, that no one can fail to be impressed. And the rest of Venice is just as absorbing. There are obvious places to visit, such as the Basilica of St Mark and the Bridge of Sighs, but just walk down any of the narrow streets – and you can go on for hours – and you will find palaces, churches, museums in abundance, all calculated to entrance the spirit. I'm beginning to sound like one of the Victorian maiden ladies I had been following, but Venice made that sort of an impression upon me.

> *But the most beautiful things of all are to be seen in the Canals and Lagoons; the burning incense turns all the sky to opal, all the Churches to pearl, all the sea to gold and crimson. Every colour gains an intensity of purity like to nothing ever seen in Northern climates.*
>
> EXTRACT FROM THE JOURNAL OF MISS M.J. FURBY

I was also much taken by the boats and the canals, and lost all fear of travelling on the water while I was there. There were so many kinds, big and small, passing to and fro, and they all had to travel at a slow speed when they were passing the buildings, to minimize the damage done by constant buffeting by waves. Except, that is, for the police boats which rush around all over the place. Another feature which interested me was all the groups of logs lashed together and poking out of the canals and the lagoon, put there I imagine, to mark the channels, and also something for the boats to tie up to. At night, particularly, they just looked like men standing in the water. Most of the time I travelled in a lovely and very luxurious launch provided by the Cipriani Hotel, where I stayed. It was quite one of the very best places I stayed at, and that is saying something when you consider the many five-star hotels I enjoyed along the way. The Cipriani is magnificently situated on an island opposite St Mark's Square and has the most attractive gardens and terraces,

The luxury of the Hotel Cipriani's launch and going at speed.

A chat with Ramot Marco, our guide in Venice, above. Whicker country! ... poolside at the Cipriani.

and the biggest hotel swimming pool I have ever seen. It also had its own little vineyard. I know it's called a millionaire's para-dise and the kind of place that Alan Whicker chooses to do his interviews (and had done precisely that a year or two ago, I understand) so I was a bit worried about the kind of person who could afford to stay there. I was very much aware I was privi-leged to be there because of a combination of good luck and a happy accident, and wondered whether my fellow guests

Strolling towards the pool at the Hotel Cipriani.

would be the friendly sort. So I put on a new dress and gave the cameo brooch and gold chain which I had bought on the Ponte Vecchio in Florence its first airing, and went to sit by the pool. But my fears were groundless, because guests and staff alike were charming – indeed, I was even recognized by a very nice couple from London who stopped for a chat whenever they saw me and wanted to know everything about my tour.

The hotel launch was available on request any time of the day

or night to go to the main part of Venice, and it also conveyed parties to various places of interest. There are scores of islands in what I call the inland sea around Venice, the most popular being Murano, which is famous for Venetian glass. I joined a trip to go there, and I was quite amazed when we were passing the island they used for a cemetery to be told that Johann Strauss was buried there. I couldn't imagine him leaving his beloved Vienna, although I knew he spent some time in America and wrote about his eagerness to get back home. It seems he spent the last years of his life in Venice and I would be very interested to know the reasons which decided him to come to live there.

They were so kind to me when I visited the Cenedese glass-works on Murano, and the manager himself, a Mr Antonio Camatti, escorted me with much courtesy throughout the after-noon I spent there. He told me that glass had been made in Venice since AD 982, but the makers decided to transfer every-thing to Murano in the second century AD because – would you believe – of commercial espionage. An island afforded much more security. I watched as one of the craftsmen made a piece in front of a furnace giving out a tremendous heat. I can't imagine how he manages to do it at the height of summer. It was obvious that it must take years to acquire the skill that he displayed. He kept on blowing down a pipe to alter the shape, then placed it back into the flames several times. I thought it was going to be a red vase, but it turned out to be a green plate, beautifully fashioned. Then I was taken on a tour of the showroom, which went on and on, room after room, and they were all full of trea-sures. Every kind of glassware you can imagine and every colour combination possible. If I had to pick on just one piece as my favourite, it might have been a superb, gold-trimmed chande-lier, made from over a thousand pieces. But then, it was so enor-mous you would have needed a pretty large palace to display it, and it was priced at around fifty thousand pounds!

Obviously the Cenedese firm had a special reputation for quality because it was chosen to be honoured by a visit by Prince Charles and other royals, and Mr Camatti was most anxious to show me the photographs taken on those occasions. I wasn't able to buy the green plate I had watched being made, because everything fresh from the furnace has to be matured in a special

In the showrooms of the Murano glass factory.

place for at least a day, so I left empty-handed. But just before I left Venice, a package turned up at the hotel for me – the plate itself, sent by special delivery with the compliments of Mr Camatti. It now has a place of honour in Belle Vue Cottage.

On the way back from Murano, the launch took me on a lovely trip around the lagoon, specifically to show me another island, Burano, which is famous for its rows of houses painted in harmonious shades of pastel colours. I also saw a market in full swing in the square by the church and watched fishermen mending their nets. There was a spectacular sunset on the way back to the hotel, and since we were well away from any habitation, our launch was able to travel at full speed, throwing up a spray which sparkled in the dying rays of the sun. Every now and again, another boat would cross our path at speed and send out waves which caused us to bounce about, which I found exciting – a new experience. Yes, Venice made me revise my opinion of boats completely and I won't be so nervous of them in the future. Of course it is necessary to spend a fair proportion of your time afloat if you wish to see Venice properly and it has a curious effect. Even when I wasn't in the boat it felt as though the ground was moving. It was surprising. I had heard about sailors walking with a rolling gait after a long time at sea, so now I know why!

Of course, the most famous boat on the waters of Venice is the gondola, and no trip to this magic place can be considered complete without a ride in one. They have been there for centuries.

> *Those gondolas are the perfection of locomotion as they glide along the silent, still and tranquil waters . . . and everywhere you hear music and song.*
>
> EXTRACT FROM THE JOURNAL OF MISS M.J. FURBY

My gondola was very beautiful, all gleaming black lacquer with brass eagles set in the sides, and upholstered in red. The gondolier, who was very friendly and quite handsome, told me it was brand new, and that he was the third generation of his family to earn a living this way. He only had one oar to propel the boat, and I don't know how he managed to steer it so skilfully when we travelled down some of the narrower canals, which were

The glories of a
gondola ride in Venice.

very crowded in places, with gondolas full of tourists all mixed up with commercial boats delivering goods to shops and hotels.

> *You hear only the soft dip of the oars, or the sharper splash*
> *which means steering and turning, as the boat shoots*
> *forward, a touch and it stops; a twist of the wrist and it*
> *swerves aside just in time to escape the prow of a sister*
> *boat shooting from one narrow canal to another.*

EXTRACT FROM THE JOURNAL OF MISS M.J. FURBY

Yes, exactly the same thing happened to me. They are so clever at their job these gondoliers, and missed colliding by inches on many occasions. Progress could be very slow at times, particularly when about a dozen gondolas were trying to get round a corner at the same time. It was a lot easier when we emerged on to the wide open spaces of the Grand Canal, and I was taken to admire the Rialto Bridge, which is a wonderful thing and full of shops selling souvenirs. Close by is Venice's famous Fish Market where I had been taken on a tour of inspection earlier on. That occasion was my only unpleasant memory of Venice. I cannot stand the sight, and particularly the smell, of fish. I always rush past the fishmongers in Barnard Castle holding my nose, and it was rather embarrassing when I tried to walk round the endless stalls just by the Rialto. The stench was overpowering and I had to run out to find some fresh air or I would have been sick. So I looked the other way when the gondola passed by, and began the most spectacular part of the ride.

> *Down the Grand Canal what a world of beauty greets you.*
> *On each side rise Palaces of the grandest architectural*
> *perfection. Here comes the wide span of the Rialto, bearing*
> *its shops crowded with barbaric jewellery and luscious*
> *fruit. Here is the Palazzo of the Falieri where . . . if you*
> *like to believe your soft-tongued Gondolier, stands the*
> *house where Othello lived and Desdemona died. It is*
> *historically true that in the Palazzo Mocenigo, Lord Byron*
> *lived and wrote, loved and suffered.*

EXTRACT FROM THE JOURNAL OF MISS M.J. FURBY

I too saw the house where Lord Byron stayed because it has a plaque on the side to commemorate the fact. It is said that he once swam across the Grand Canal, but I was told that anyone trying to emulate that feat today would end up in hospital in the intensive care unit because the water is so polluted. But the palaces and churches are just as dazzling to the eye as they were in Byron's time – or Miss Furby's, for that matter.

Shortly after Hannah was poled under the Rialto Bridge there was an incident which confirmed, if confirmation was required, her celebrity status. At the time the Yorkshire Television crew was busily filming Hannah sitting alone in her glistening gondola when faint cries of 'Hannah! Hannah!' were heard. Looking around, a *vaporetto*, one of the water-buses which ply along the Grand Canal, was spotted, crowded to the hilt as usual with tourists. At least half a dozen people had forced their way to the side nearest to Hannah and were shouting, waving and taking photographs.

Well, that was a real surprise. My hearing, not to mention my wits, is not what it was, so some time elapsed before I realized what was going on. I know I had been recognized all over Europe, but this occasion was really rather special. It had everyone along the Grand Canal looking at me and wondering who on earth I was. Anyway, I enjoyed it and waved back and smiled for the cameras. It altogether enhanced a truly memorable journey down the rest of that amazing waterway.

The weather was reasonably benign during Hannah's stay in Venice, mixed between warm sunshine and overcast skies. The umbrella was not required for any reason – until the last night. Hannah had planned a musical farewell to the Queen of the Adriatic by taking tea in St Mark's Square on the elegant terrace outside Florian's, one of the most celebrated cafés in the world which has an orchestra of very high quality indeed. There are other excellent cafés in the same area, a couple with orchestras, but none has the style and excellence of Florian's. The murals and mirrors inside Florian's are probably priceless, but the best way to enjoy a visit there is to sit outside under a balmy Venetian evening sky, watching it turn opal and then crimson gold, to quote Miss Furby, taking

tea and fancy cakes, and listening to the music. Hannah came early
to secure a place near the bandstand, and the night sky certainly
started in classic fashion. But half an hour before the orchestra was
due to begin, the promising sunset was superseded by iron-grey
clouds which swiftly turned jet black. A ripple of thunder rolled
across the lagoon, and as the lights were switched on around the
square they were complemented by flashes of lightning. All the
potential customers fled back to their hotels, but Hannah quietly
ignored the threat, and provided a remarkable shot for the camera
– just Hannah, sitting contentedly in a sea of empty tables and
chairs, an echoing, deserted square stretching into the distance,
waiting patiently for the musicians to arrive.

Well, what else could I expect? That thunderstorm had followed
me all the way round Italy, and I suppose it had to turn up to say
goodbye. But it transpired to be a marvellous experience, nevertheless. The rain held off for quite a long time and the orchestra
turned up, and played just for me at first. They started with the
'Thunder and Lightning' polka by Johann Strauss – wonderful!
Some other tourists ventured out for a while, including a couple
from Tyneside who came over for a chat.

They were such talented players and so polite – acknow-
ledging my applause between each number and laughing a lot.
They considerably outnumbered the audience at this particular
juncture, and they obviously appreciated the humour of the
situation. Nor did they stop when the heavens did eventually
open – they were fortunately under cover – so I left my seat and
took shelter to carry on listening. I said goodbye to each one at
the end, and they responded most charmingly.

So . . . it was an unforgettable conclusion to my romance with
Venice – and a romance it most certainly was. I did not want to
leave that place. It was the last city on my Grand Tour, and it
went straight to the top of my list of favourites.

12

Homeward Bound ... by the Only Way to Travel

Homeward bound . . . and the Innocent Abroad went in a most fitting manner to round off such an odyssey. Aboard the most romantic train in history, beloved of nobility, spies, murderers (if only fictional), crime writers . . . and maiden ladies.

The Orient Express.

Even before the train set off from the station, positioned close by a Venetian canal – it must be one of the few occasions you hail a boat to catch a train – the atmosphere was charged with excitement, and the reception area where the fortunate passengers check in, airport-style, looked like a film-set ready for a re-make of *Murder on the Orient Express*. Extravagantly clad, bejewelled and coiffured ladies moved elegantly around, escorted by gentlemen who did their best to match, sartorially, while stewards, dressed in their immaculate royal-blue uniforms trimmed with gold, danced attendance and whipped matching sets of expensive luggage to the private cabins. Everything about the Venice Simplon-Orient Express, to give the train its full title, is designed to create a unique aura.

Hannah entered upon this scene in all her own finery, underpinned by sensible shoes, and fitted in perfectly, even if she was more of an Agatha Christie, or maybe a Miss Marple figure than a Mata Hari, *femme fatale* type, but fully at ease, nevertheless. By this stage of her tour she was becoming a seasoned traveller, moving into new situations with much more confidence and aplomb. She allowed herself to be swept along, no longer fearful of whether she would be accepted by her sophisticated fellow passengers.

I cannot imagine a better way to travel – the only way, if you can afford it. It's an overwhelming experience. So much has been written about the Orient Express, so many films and television programmes, that I wondered if the reality would match the expectation generated by all that publicity. But it exceeded it in every way. The magic begins long before you climb aboard, with all kinds of fascinating people milling around dressed in clothes you only usually see in fashion magazines. Everyone had clearly gone to a lot of trouble to make it a memorable occasion – of course, for most it must be a once-in-a-lifetime experience.

A 1929 poster
advertising the Simplon
Orient Express.
*Compagnie Internationale
des Wagons-Lits et du
Tourisme*

Preparing to board the
Orient Express.

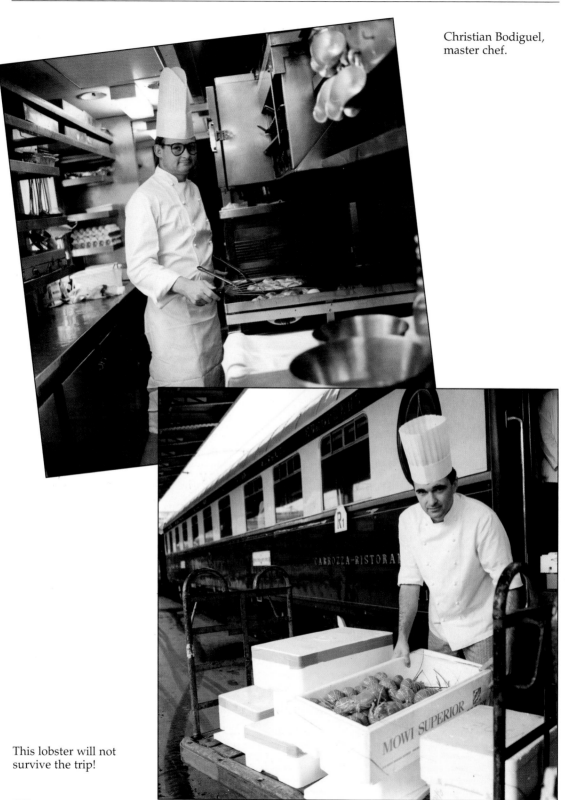

Christian Bodiguel,
master chef.

This lobster will not
survive the trip!

As for the train itself, well, it must have been entirely constructed by master craftsmen. Every carriage was an antique from the original Orient Express, tracked down and bought by the new owners and faithfully restored in every detail. All the woodwork has been inlaid with exquisite marquetry, the cabins are the last word in luxury, and everything – inside and out – gleams as though it has just been polished. Which it probably has – they even wash and rub down the exterior of the train after every journey so that it is spotless each time it sets off again.

All the people I met were kind and friendly, passengers and staff alike. Each carriage had a steward, who was at your beck and call every moment of the day and night. Mine was a very obliging young man called Frank, who came from Glasgow. And when it turned out that the main course for lunch, the first big event, was veal, which I will not eat, the head chef did me a beefsteak just the way I like it, cooked properly all the way through. He was called Christian Bodiguel, a very intense young Frenchman with a big reputation in his profession, who had worked in some of the top Parisian restaurants. He was a most persuasive gentleman, too. When I tried to decline the fish course at dinner because the memory of that visit to the Fish Market in Venice was still fresh (if that is the word!), he assured me that the way he cooked it would remove any fishy odour, and he was as good as his word. I really enjoyed it. He was also agreeable about the dessert, which was peaches and wild cherries cooked in kirsch. He prepared one without the alcohol, just for me.

The journey was really one long party. People drank champagne cocktails in the superbly appointed bar before dinner, then returned afterwards for coffee, more drinks and conversation and to listen to a very talented pianist at a grand piano until well into the night. And the life and soul of the party as far as I was concerned turned out to be another Yorkshirewoman. I first noticed her when we were checking in at the station in Venice – everybody did, because she was wearing a lovely, long creation all in white with the most amazing pearl necklace. It had scores and scores of tiny pearls spraying out in all directions, like little drops of white water. She looked wonderful, and was clearly determined to enjoy every second of the ride – and did! Julie Ste-

The luxury of the original Wagon-Lits trains has not faded, above. A poster advertising Wagon-Lits travel, below. *Compagnie Internationale des Wagon-Lits et du Tourisme*

phenson was her name, and she and her husband, David, created fun and laughter wherever they went. They hailed from Dewsbury and she told me she was a sculptress and painter. She must be a very accomplished artist because I understand one of her sculptures is displayed in York Minster.

The Stephensons became firm friends of another jolly couple, Peter and Anne Copeland from Brighton, and together they made my journey much more pleasurable by being so friendly and interested in me. We all talked and made merry for hours after dinner and Julie even talked me – much against my inclinations – into playing the piano before I retired to my bed. At somewhere around one in the morning!

Sheer luxury – relaxing in my cabin on the Orient Express.

Julie Stephenson may have been the star of the trip, but Hannah, in her own, quiet way turned just as many heads and she was

approached several times by admirers, including a couple from Australia. The grand climax of the party was Hannah's performance on the piano. It took a great deal of persuasion to get her in front of the keys, and she was momentarily baffled to find it had three pedals, a refinement she had never previously encountered. And her style – particularly when compared with the stylish professional who preceded her – was decidedly homely and old-fashioned, but she played for a good ten minutes and finished to enthusiastic applause, which she graciously acknowledged.

Me, Caroline Rathbone and the life and soul of the party, Julie Stephenson.

Well, they were very generous because I know I'm not very good. But it certainly ended the evening on a high note for me, if not such a melodious one for my audience. I slept soundly because I was very tired after such a late night and all that excitement. In the morning, Frank, my steward, served me with a light breakfast in my cabin – but that was just the prelude to what they called a brunch, served at 10.30 a.m. What a spread it was, for so early in the day. Scrambled eggs with smoked salmon, followed by a whole lobster with a potato creation, all topped off for dessert by a caramelized apple tart done in the French fashion. But I couldn't face up to it, grand though it was, after all the indulgence of the day before – although I must confess everyone else seemed to be delighted. But Christian the chef was kind to me once again and served up a tasty salad with the potato. I also had the rolls and butter, something I enjoyed at breakfast all the way through Europe.

By that time, the Orient Express had left Paris and we were heading towards the Channel on the same line we had travelled at the start of the trip, except in the opposite direction, of course. And the scenery had definitely taken a turn for the worse, especially when compared with the wonderful views as we sped through the mountains and lakes of Italy and Switzerland. I had a slight but distinct feeling of despondency because the end of the line was in sight, in more ways than one. Another two or three hours and we would be back in Britain.

The final filmed interview of many was conducted as the train neared Boulogne, when Hannah reviewed the highlights of her odyssey.

I am very sorry it is coming to an end because it has, with very few exceptions, been absolutely marvellous. Lovely places, lovely people. There are, of course, parts which stand out in the memory, such as the thrill of walking down the Champs-Elysées . . . and the Paris Opera House was very special. Then the Rhine cruise with Lisa . . . Vienna will also be very close to my heart, always, and I still remember those gardens with that wonderful statue of Johann Strauss . . . Pompeii, of course, and the visit to Fulvia's home in Naples . . . those vine-growers in Tuscany where the views and the buildings were so outstanding. And Venice . . . that was in a category of its own, the icing on the cake.

Nor must I forget the dogs I met along the way. I missed having my own dog around and often wondered how my little Timmy was getting on. Trouble was, I had to be a bit cautious about touching dogs over here because of the risk of rabies.

If there is one place I wouldn't rush back to it would be the

Alps, although I understand perfectly well their appeal to other people. I did appreciate their grandeur, but there is no way I would go on a winter sports holiday unless all I had to do was sit in a nice hotel in front of a warm fire and listen to Austrian music.

The worst part of the trip?

The weather. It rained so much, and it was so cold at times.

The worst experience?

Going into the Blue Grotto in that little boat.

And, when asked the final question – 'If there was just one place you could pick to return to, which would it be?' – the reply was instantaneous.

Venice!

Yes, I did suggest that I should stay on the Orient Express when I found out it was returning to Venice from Boulogne at 5.00 p.m. on the afternoon we sailed. The very agreeable people who run the train said they would be glad to have me, but otherwise my request fell on deaf ears!

However, there was plenty of enjoyment to come after we arrived at Folkstone – and there was a special area on the boat for Orient Express passengers – because another train, just as splendidly appointed, was waiting to take us to London. It was made up of Pullman carriages, all different designs, and some had carried royalty. We were served a delicious afternoon tea and plenty of it, including scones, jam and clotted cream just to remind us we were back in the home country. It was also good to taste real tea again, too.

But . . . oh dear! . . . boarding the 1.40 from Euston wasn't the same as catching the 10.40 from Venice. I went to Carlisle first to stay with Kathy Rooney and sort myself out before returning to Cotherstone.

It was nice, of course, to get back to Belle Vue Cottage and

Lunch with Caroline Rathbone, a publicity executive with the Orient Express.

End of the line ...
leaving the Orient
Express at Boulogne.

meet up with Timmy and all my friends again. Timmy was fine, if a little subdued at first, and the ladies of the village were anxious to hear about my experiences.

Nothing had changed. The hall was full of mail, people began knocking on my door again, wanting to meet me and have the books autographed, and the telephone kept ringing with invitations to make appearances here, there and everywhere.

Which was nice, of course. But . . . I felt queer. I think I've become something of a displaced person.

I didn't want it to end.

13

The Perils of Foreign Travel –
Lifts, Locks and Lavatories …
and the Beginning of Europe's
First Good Porridge Guide

For the first-time traveller abroad there are many pitfalls along the way, but for an innocent like Hannah Hauxwell, who is as sweetly unworldly as any person in Britain, possibly Europe, there were recurring problems on several themes. This charming naivety can be best illustrated by the incident not so many years ago when Hannah was confronted by her first set of revolving doors. It happened on her initial visit to Yorkshire Television's headquarters in Leeds, when her escort stepped politely aside to allow her to proceed through the revolving doors into the foyer. He was mystified for a few moments when she stood stock-still and gazed with much puzzlement at this unusual contraption, then realized that she had neither seen nor heard of such a thing. So he leaned forward and set them in motion, whereupon Hannah beamed with surprise and delight and exclaimed, 'Oh, what a marvellous idea!' She soon learned to master the intricacies of revolving doors, but throughout her tour of Europe she fought a running battle with lifts, locks and lavatories, and was particularly frustrated in her efforts to obtain a decent pot of tea. But she did return with the beginnings of a new culinary enterprise, the First Good Porridge Guide to Europe.

Travel accessory advertisement from 1909.
British Museum/Fotomas

Old posters advertising
Thomas Cook tours.
*Courtesy of Thomas Cook
Archives*

I must have lost quite a bit of weight because of the various lifts I encountered. Lifts are not to my liking really, so if there is no one to take me up or down, then I always choose to use the stairs, often several times a day, and if my room was on one of the upper floors it was a grand way to shed a few pounds. They all seemed to be different, too, with such complicated controls. And because I like to consider the situation for a moment or two before getting in, the doors either closed before I could get across the threshold, or just as I put one foot inside. They also vary in size, and if I had been a few inches wider I wouldn't have been able to get into the one in the hotel we stayed in in Florence. Someone like Cyril Smith would have found it totally impossible, it was so narrow. I noticed it caused endless confusion among the other guests, particularly if they were carrying some hand luggage, and after a couple of very crowded experiences I declined to enter it, even if there was someone to look after me.

Another problem for me centred around locks, starting with the doors in the hotels. It is unbelievable how many variations they have dreamt up to secure your bedroom door. Some just lock automatically, some have levers, some have a kind of button arrangement, and you never knew whether any of them went either up or down, clockwise or anti-clockwise. No, I couldn't fathom a lot of them and often gave up trying and went to bed with the door unlocked. But my biggest worry centred round the various ladies' rooms I used, especially at the service stations we stopped at on the Italian motorways. It is a revelation what you have to push or what you have to pull and some of the locks were very dubious contraptions. I went into one toilet and turned something, then couldn't get the blinking thing loose when I wanted to leave. In the end I got rather worried and began rattling the door to try and attract some attention, and it was only by chance that I pushed something and it opened. That was a bit frightening so ever afterwards I was very wary and tested every lock first before committing myself.

Then there were the holes in the ground. One look, and I refused to have anything further to do with those things. And I was rather surprised to see a woman at the entrance to most toilets who expected you to put a coin on a saucer. Since I tend to

Uniformed interpreters on international railway stations are a thing of the past! *Courtesy of Thomas Cook Archives*

Enjoying lunch in a Salzburg
restaurant, above.
An Orient Express dinner menu
from 1884, below.
*Compagnie Internationale des Wagons-
Lits et du Tourisme*

use ladies' rooms more often than most, I must have spent a tidy sum in the end.

Hannah also failed to acclimatize to the various styles of Continental cuisine sampled in the five countries she visited. But she rarely missed enjoying three square meals a day. Whenever a head count for a trip out to dinner after the conclusion of the day's filming was taken, Hannah never cried off. While others opted to return exhausted to their rooms and order a sandwich, she was always eager to go. She had some difficulty negotiating the various menus and left many puzzled waiters in her wake, but she always ended up with a plateful of whatever simple, non-spicy fare they could produce, and ate up everything. Desserts were easier, except those containing alcohol or cheese, and she stuck rigidly to water whenever offered a drink.

Some of the food I liked, except for the pasta in Italy, although I noticed a tendency which is becoming widespread in our own country for only half cooking things. Mostly I avoided red meat and stuck to fish and chicken. Nor would I touch veal, which

With the film crew at the café on the Mer de Glace in Switzerland.

seemed to be on most menus on the Continent, because it comes from little calves. Trying to obtain a decent cup of tea was a continuing problem. Mostly they brought some lukewarm water and a separate teabag, plus a slice of lemon, but no milk. And by the time I had managed to make them understand that I wanted milk, the water was practically stone cold. In Naples, I think the cow had gone dry, and I ended up using the lemon. Nor do I like the habit of not spreading butter on the bread, which spoiled a few good ham sandwiches for me. But some of the puddings were very tasty – I have something of a sweet tooth – and I also developed a liking for cappuccino coffee in Italy. But my main concern in the morning, after establishing what the tea was like, was to see if I could get any porridge. Now I am partial to porridge because it's a really good start to the day, and I don't often cook it at home because it makes such a mess of the pan. From the Rhine trip onwards I tried to order it with every breakfast. It was lovely Lisa's idea – the German lady who became such a good friend on the boat – that I should have it one morning

Sunshine breakfast on the terrace at the Cipriani Hotel in Venice.

because I had indicated to her in some way, probably by sign language since we didn't share a common tongue, that I was feeling a little under the weather. Lisa made it clear that porridge would do me good and I think she was trying to tell me that her father had been a doctor and he had always recommended it, so I took her advice – and it worked. Very good it was, too, and quite a lot superior to some I tasted later on. A lot of Continental porridge is what I call crowdy – not creamy enough – and it wasn't always possible to obtain enough milk to thin it down a little. In some places, such as Naples, porridge was nonexistent, but in Rome they managed to find me some even though it wasn't on the menu. The two top places for porridge in my experience can be found in Siena, where it was brought to me in a lovely big silver tureen, and in Venice, where on the Cipriani Hotel breakfast buffet there must have been nearly a gallon of the most excellent quality, kept nicely warm in another tureen.

Acknowledgements and thanks ...

First and foremost to Kathy Rooney, Hannah Hauxwell and Barry Cockcroft extend much gratitude for her indispensable services as friend, production co-ordinator, transcriber and typist, and general solver of problems across five nations.

Sincere thanks are also extended to all the people who feature in this book, some of whom will probably be surprised to discover they do so, and to those who worked so hard behind the scenes to bring a complex operation to a successful conclusion, namely:

David Holden, Nigel Pearce, Edmund Swinglehurst, Joy Hooper, Derek Tetmar and Jill Weston of Thomas Cook Ltd., Peter Gillbe of Optomen Television, Emilio Tommasi (Director) and Eugenio Magnani of the Italian State Tourist Office in London, Anna Maria Rubera and Zeffiro Riccetti of RAI in Rome, Lando Gonnelli in Florence, Edoardo Moretti in Pisa, Federigo Sani in Siena, Francisco Bianchi in Naples, Franco Natalino in Pompeii, Elio Sica in Capri, Cesare Battisti, Ramot Marco and Natale Rusconi in Venice, Marc Humphries of the French Government Tourist Office in London, Michele Roucaute and Monique de Bonnerive in Paris, Agatha Seuss of the German Tourist Office in London, Annamarie van Assendelft in Rüdesheim am Rhein, Astrid Sappler of the Austrian Tourist Office in London, Roswitha Holz in Salzburg, Traudl Lisey in Vienna, Heidi Reisz and Evelyn Lafone of the Swiss National Tourist Office in London, Ann Forrer in Lenk, Rupert Brown and Julie Mitchell of British Rail in London, Nadia Stancioff and Caroline Rathbone of Orient Express Hotels, Philip Esclasse of Sealink Ferries, Richard Webster in Norwich, Bob and Irene Tilmouth in Tyne and Wear, Yvonne Drury, Grant McKee, Sue Hamelman, Chris Sutton, Nick Gray, Mel Bradley, Brian Jeeves, Hilary Arnold, Sophie Figgis, Valerie Buckingham, Barbara Bagnall, Louise Weir, Frances Johnson, Helen Everson, Behram Kapadia, Carol Hainstock, Roy Bolton, Vivien Green . . . and John Fairley.

SPECIAL THANKS . . . to Mostafa Hammuri, for the skill and dedication unfailingly displayed in assembling an outstanding portfolio of stills which enhance this book.

Mostafa is an internationally celebrated film cameraman who joined Yorkshire Television more than twenty years ago. An award winner, he shot the first, momentous documentary about Hannah, 'Too Long A Winter' and he has worked on Barry Cockcroft's programmes consistently ever since.

In recent years, Mostafa has established an outstanding new reputation as a stills photographer, providing the illustrations for the Hauxwell/Cockcroft books, and other publications.